KU-285-637

Essentials of
PROJECT
CONTROL

Essentials of
PROJECT
CONTROL

EDITORS' CHOICE SERIES

Series Editors:
Jeffrey K. Pinto
Jeffrey W. Trailer

Project Management Institute

Library of Congress Cataloging-in-Publication Data

Essentials of project control / edited by Jeffrey K. Pinto, Jeffrey W.
  Trailer
      p.   cm.   --   (Vol. 2 in the Editors' choice series from PMI)
     Articles selected from Project management journal and PM network.
     Includes bibliographical references.
     ISBN: 1–880410–64–8 (pbk. : alk. paper)
     1. Industrial project management. I. Pinto, Jeffrey K.
II. Trailer, Jeffrey W. III. Project Management Institute.
IV. Project management journal. V. PM network. VI. Series:
Editors' choice series ; vol. 2.
HD69.P75E85   1999
658.4'04 – – dc21   99–41753
                                         CIP

ISBN: 1-880410-64-8

Published by: Project Management Institute, Inc.
        Four Campus Boulevard
        Newtown Square, Pennsylvania 19073-3299 USA
        Phone: 610-356-4600 or Visit our website: www.pmi.org

Copyright ©1999 Project Management Institute, Inc. All rights reserved.

"PMI" is a trade and service mark registered in the United States and other nations; "PMP" and the PMP logo are registered certification marks in the United States and other nations; "PMBOK" is a trademark registered in the United States and other nations; and the PMI logo, "PM Network," "Project Management Journal," "PMI Today," and "Building professionalism in project management." are trademarks of Project Management Institute, Inc.

Printed in the United States of America. No part of this work may be reproduced or transmitted in any form or by any means, electronic, manual, photocopying, recording, or by any information storage and retrieval system, without prior written permission of the publisher.

PMI® books are available at quantity discounts. For more information, please write to the Publisher, PMI Publishing, Four Campus Boulevard, Newtown Square, PA 19073-3299 USA. Call: (610) 356-4600 or visit your local bookstore.

The paper used in this book complies with the Permanent Paper Standard issued by the National Information Standards Organization (Z39.48-1984).

10 9 8 7 6 5 4 3

Table of Contents

Figures and Tables

Scope Creep ...
Not Necessarily a Bad Thing

S. Craig Keifer, PMP

PM Network (May 1996)

This article was first published in the October 1995 issue of
the Western Michigan PMI Chapter Newsletter, *On Target*.

W E HAVE ALL heard horror stories of a project's scope growing
out of control, and more than a few of us have lived through
such experiences. Timing gets later and later, costs keep growing,
management is unhappy, and customers are dissatisfied. Essentially,
more work than originally planned is added to a program, and the
project cannot absorb it without missing one or more objectives (or
passing up opportunities). In the latter stages of a project, when
changes require modifications to hard tools or brick and mortar, scope
creep is obvious. But in the early stages, a project's scope can easily
grow through changes in customer wants, miscommunication, poor
assumptions, and successive minor additions to design. Even though
scope creep can be devastating to a project, the pressure to increase
the scope of a project will always be there and, if properly managed,
provides significant opportunities for the performing organization.

Scope creep can be defined as the slow, insidious growth of a
project beyond its original work content and objectives. Several key
indicators put up *red flags* when scope starts to creep. But because
these same red flags can also be indicative of other problems in the
project, take care when reaching a conclusion as to the root cause
of a particular condition.

One of the key indicators is, of course, project timing. When timing starts to slip for no identifiable reason, growth in the scope of the program should be suspected. Similarly, if the project budget starts to overrun, without other identified reasons, you should determine if more work is being done than was originally agreed to and budgeted.

CHANGE = OPPORTUNITY

Major changes in project direction are usually well recognized and accounted for, but day-to-day interaction with your customer results in many small compounding refinements to the project direction. Properly recognized and properly handled, these can represent an opportunity for your organization to increase sales, build a reputation, and solidify relationships.

- Adding content to your final product can enhance sales—and profits. If addressed appropriately and incorporated only after assessing its impact on the rest of the project's objectives, every change represents a pricing opportunity.
- Some changes, while they may not provide a direct product-pricing opportunity, may well provide the chance to demonstrate to your customer and other potential customers the capabilities of your organization. This positions you for future business with the current customer and also enhances your company's reputation in the industry. Such changes must be well evaluated in terms of the cost versus the anticipated benefit.
- Even at increased cost, absorption of some changes may benefit the development of a long-term relationship with your customer. Helping your customers get their jobs done usually helps you get your job done! Again, any such changes need to be evaluated in the context of the present and projected long-term relationship.

CHANGE CAN DRIVE YOU NUTS

Among the primary sources of scope creep, one of the clearest is the continual refinement of product direction. In the automotive industry, projects are often initiated with very minimal definition of the final product. Even when a fairly good initial definition exists, the product evolves through the development process with successive additions and changes to design features, colors, materials, option complexity, and so forth.

Assumptions regarding the development process and the relative responsibilities are also refined as the project proceeds. As confusion about who is responsible for various aspects (e.g., testing, documentation) and to what level each task needs to be performed (e.g., types of tests, level of drawing or CAD detail) is clarified, it impacts the performing organization's ability to achieve its internal and customer objectives.

Large customer organizations with various supporting departments may not develop requirements in time to support the initial definition of work. Yet these requirements will subsequently be universally applied to all suppliers or contractors. Because the requiring department doesn't deal directly with the suppliers in a timing and pricing mode, these additional requirements may be issued as a decree, leaving others to sort out the implications.

If the customer organization cannot complete its tasks on time to support you, it may be necessary to *help out*. Taking on additional tasks because it's the only way to keep the project moving at the required pace builds relationships and demonstrates capability, but, unfortunately, it's difficult to convert such changes into additional sales.

Whether major shifts in direction or minor refinements to the present course of the project, changes should be implemented in the least disruptive way possible, retaining the maximum opportunity to meet project objectives (either original or revised). This means complete evaluation of the impacts on the total project, not just on the immediate task. A review of project-level cost and timing is, of course, a first step, but the implications to project risk must also be considered. For example, in the automotive industry, where vehicle builds are scheduled years in advance and thousands of suppliers are all working to the same deadline, a change to your project schedule that consumes all available schedule contingency prior to the vehicle builds should be looked at as a substantial risk. Missing a vehicle build is not an alternative, so eliminating schedule contingency increases the risk that compression costs (overtime, expedited freight, and priority rates) will be needed if any critical tasks exceed their duration estimates.

When dealing with these changes, don't overlook the impact on the project team. Frequent or significant changes in direction or tear-ups in design have a demoralizing effect on all the people involved. No matter how dedicated, a team's energy, creativity, and enthusiasm wanes when its members begin to feel that they have completed the same task three or four times. Factor in the human aspect when considering changes of any level.

So much for some of the causes, effects, and opportunities of scope changes; now, let's examine some guidelines for controlling scope change and implementing scope creep as an opportunity and not a risk.

Control Is the Key

First, it is vitally important to establish a written, detailed baseline. The baseline should encompass both the final products and the work process that will be used to deliver that product. In some industries, a quotation package or a formal contract would determine the baseline. In the automotive industry, under the present philosophy of early supplier selection, the product may not be well defined at the time that you are selected as a supplier and expected to commit to some form of cost and timing. This puts more pressure on you to delineate what you intend to provide and all the assumptions used to develop your costs and timing. Although this baseline will probably not represent the final product and process, it does represent the starting point or *stake in the ground* from which all scope changes can be tracked.

Your customers need to be well informed of the content of your baseline, as any discrepancies between what you think you are selling and what they think they are buying need to be resolved as early as possible. A joint agreement on the stake in the ground is crucial to assure appropriate incorporation of subsequent changes, as well as to prevent major disagreements over pricing at a later stage in the project.

When establishing the baseline with your customer, also establish how the baseline will be changed. All changes should be documented in a format acceptable to both your own organization and your customer organization. This reduces the total workload necessary for completing multiple forms for the same change and also eliminates a potential for translation error. The format should be individually tailored to the particulars of your own organization, the customer organization, and to the project. Thus, though some differences may exist from project to project within your organization, the overall communication on a particular project will be maximized. Even though additional, more formal documentation may be required later (such as purchase-order modifications), a joint direction and communication document maintains the pace of the project.

A change document should include all significant factors. For most projects, this includes items such as project costs, investment in tooling and facilities, product costs, and timing. However, specific projects or industries may have other requirements that must also be closely tracked (product weight, environmental concerns, risk levels). By including all of the significant factors (with justifications), the product-change documentation becomes a stand-alone document that requires no further explanation. All variances should be measured against the present approved level of the baseline.

When defining the change documentation format, the individuals with the responsibility for authorizing the change must be identified. This authority may be different, depending on the nature or level of the change, and it may mean that more than one individual from each organization must be involved. It is imperative that authorizing individuals for both organizations acknowledge (sign) the change document so that the document can be recognized as official direction.

After approval of a change, two significant tasks must be completed. The first is the updating of the baseline to incorporate the changes. The updated baseline is then used as the basis for any future changes. All change documents should be retained so that the project-change history can be traced from the initiation of the project to the termination, and postproject analyses can use this history as a guide for future similar projects.

Finally, the change must be communicated to all parties involved in the project so that the entire team is working toward the same direction. Slow dissemination of direction changes causes confusion on the project team, with subsequent loss of efficiency and morale. Everyone needs to be working on the same thing, with the most up-to-date direction.

Changes to the work content and objectives of a project, whether small creeping changes or large shifts in direction, are to be expected. With careful attention to detail, changes can be implemented as opportunities for the performing organization. Recognizing the sources and impact of changes and instituting appropriate controlling measures ensures that a project meets all of its objectives.

Best Practices for Controlling Technology-Based Projects

Hans J. Thamhain, Bentley College, Waltham, Massachusetts

Project Management Journal (Dec. 1996)

CHALLENGES OF MANAGING PROJECTS TODAY

For world-class companies, project management is a powerful competitive tool, crucial for achieving desired business performance (Berman and Vasconcellos 1994; Raz 1993; Thamhain 1994b). Although the basic concepts of project management have been known for a long time (Randolph and Posner 1988; Thamhain and Wilemon, 1986), its discipline expands continuously (Knutson 1996). As a result, the tools, techniques, and management practices needed to run projects successfully in today's challenging business environment have changed considerably (Cespedes 1994; Clark and Wheelwright 1992a; Davis 1994; Ramping up 1995; Hofman and Rochart 1992; Moder 1994; Thamhain 1994b). Until the 1980s, project management focused on administrating schedule and resource data. This tracking of project metrics is still an important part of project management (Cunningham 1994; Rigby 1995; Thamhain and Wilemon 1986). However, the business environment of the 1990s is quite different from what it used to be. New technologies have become a significant factor for almost every business, affecting project activities from small to large and from service to manufacturing (Berman and Vasconcellos 1994; Deschamps and Nayak 1995; Rigby 1995; Thamhain 1996b). Computers and communications have radically changed the workplace and have transformed our global economy more and more toward service and knowledge work with a high mobility of resources, skills, processes, and technology itself.

Technology—What Is Different? Despite the difficulty of measuring *technology content* of a business, or separating high-technology from low-technology projects, many managers clearly identify their projects as *high technology*. They see themselves in a different, more challenging environment. When describing their operations—whether product, process, or service oriented—these managers strike some common ground. Supported by considerable research (Archibald 1992; Berman and Vasconcellos 1994; Clark and Wheelwright 1992b; DeMaio 1994; Gobeli and Brown 1993; Martinez 1995; Raz 1993; Slevin and Pinto 1987; Thamhain 1990, 1994b, 1996b; Thamhain and Wilemon 1996), these managers identify specific characteristics that make their work environment unique:

- high degrees of work complexity
- evolving solutions
- high levels of innovation and creativity
- intricate technology transfer processes
- multidisciplinary teamwork and decision-making
- complex support systems such as CAD, CAM, ERP, and DFM/A
- sophisticated multicompany alliances
- highly complex forms of work integration.

In addition, self-directed teams are gradually replacing the traditional, more hierarchically structured project team (Sprague and Greenwell 1992; Thamhain and Wilemon 1996), and are seen as a significant tool for orchestrating and eventually controlling complex projects. However, they also require a more sophisticated management style that relies strongly on group interaction, resource and power sharing, individual accountability, commitment, self-direction, and control (Bahrami 1992; Higgins and Watts 1986; Larsen and Gobeli 1987; Mintzberg 1994; Thamhain 1990). These complex projects and their integration also rely to a considerable extent on member-generated performance norms and evaluations rather than hierarchical guidelines, policies, and procedures (Thamhain and Wilemon 1996). While this paradigm shift is the result of changing organizational complexities, capabilities,

8

demands, and cultures, it also requires radical departures from traditional management philosophy on organizational structure, motivation, leadership, and project control. As a result, traditional management tools, designed largely for top-down control and centralized command and communications, are no longer sufficient for generating satisfactory results.

New Management Tools. In response to these challenges, new project management tools and techniques have evolved, which are often more integrated with the business process, offering more sophisticated capabilities for project tracking and control in an environment that is not only different in culture, but also has to deal with a broad spectrum of contemporary challenges such as time-to-market, accelerating technologies, innovation, resource limitations, technical complexities, project metrics, operational dynamics, risk, and uncertainty (Dean et al. 1992; Thamhain 1994b; Thamhain and Weiss 1992; Thomasen and Butterfield 1993). Using these modern tools requires new skills and a more sophisticated management style. All of this has a profound impact on the way project leaders must manage to get desired results. The methods of communication, decision-making, soliciting commitment, and risk sharing are constantly shifting away from a centralized, autocratic management style toward a team-centered, more self-directed form of project control (Cash and Fox 1992; Cespedes 1994; Jackman 1989/1990; Kernaghan 1986; Thamhain and Wilemon 1986). Equally important, project control has radically departed from its narrow focus of satisfying schedule and budget constraints to a much broader and more balanced managerial approach, which focuses on the effective search for solutions to complex problems (Abdel-Hamid and Madnick 1990; Dean et al. 1992; Greiner and Schein 1981; Hatfield 1995; Lewis 1990). This requires tradeoffs among many parameters such as creativity, change-orientation, quality, and traditional schedule and budget constraints (Lovitt 1996; Oberlender and Abel 1995; Tippett and Waits 1994). Control also requires accountability and commitment from the team members toward the project objectives.

WHAT WE KNOW ABOUT CONTROLLING TECHNICAL PROJECTS

The importance of project control and its impact on business performance has long been recognized (Cash and Fox 1992; Lewis

1991; Thamhain 1990a). Effective control helps run the project according to plan, often in spite of changes, contingencies, and work-related complexities especially common to technology-based businesses. Considerable research has been conducted on the methods and practices of conventional project control, related primarily to schedule and budget administration, with results extensively discussed in the literature (Anbari 1985; Archibald 1992; Cash and Fox 1992; Christensen 1994; Cunningham 1994; Drigani 1989; "1995 Project Management Software Survey"; Lewis 1991; Randolph and Posner 1988). However, conventional tools and methods of project control seldom produce satisfactory results in today's environment. Today's technology projects especially require innovative solutions to complex problems and flexible change-oriented implementation of the project plan. Traditional methods of schedule and budget control are often useless and sometimes even counterproductive to overall project performance (Anbari 1985; Cleland 1985; Lovitt 1996; Manganelli and Klein 1994; Prasad 1995; Roberts and Hughes 1996).

Competing effectively in such a complex marketplace requires more than just technological parity and resources. It also requires the ability to manage these projects through today's complex, fast-changing organizations, its people, processes, and operating systems, all working together in an intricate, integrated fashion (Bahrami 1992; Thamhain 1994b). Yet, especially for technology-intensive work, our project management systems have not kept up with the vastly changing organizational needs (Adler, McDonald and MacDonald 1992; Beacon et al. 1994; Deschamps and Nayak 1995).

Trying to Climb Out of Quandaries. On the other side, many companies in recent years have invested heavily in *new management tools and techniques* that promise more effective alternatives and enhancements to traditional forms of project control. Tables 1–3 summarize the more popular methods, including both traditional and contemporary tools used today. These tools are grouped into three categories: analytical tools and techniques, procedural tools and techniques, and people-oriented tools and techniques.

Applications overlap a great deal among these tools within each category as well as among the three classifications. However, each group provides some descriptive focus and a convenient way to partition and catalog the long list of control tools.

So much for the tool box! The problem is that these management tools do not come with users' manuals. For starters, there has

Analytical Management Technique	Description	Elements of Control	Conditions for Successful Control
Action Item/ Report	A memo or report defining specific items agreed upon with the resolver, necessary to move the project forward or to correct a deficiency.	Responsibility identification, personal commitment, peer pressure.	Individual commitment, management support, incentives.
Computer Software	Computer software to support project planning, tracking, and control. Provides various reports of project status and performance analysis, and documentation.	Schedule, budget, PERT/CPM, resource leveling scheduling, cost-time tradeoff.	Ability to measure status. Valid input data. Willingness to correct deviations. Leadership.
Critical Path Analysis	Analysis of the longest paths within a network schedule with the objective of 1) determining the impact of task delays, problems, contingencies, and organizational dependencies, 2) finding solutions, and, 3) optimizing schedule performance.	Schedule, budget, deliverables, cost-time tradeoff.	Accurate estimates of effort, cost, and duration.
Budget Tracking	Analysis of planned versus actual budget expenditures relative to work performed. The objective is to detect and correct project performance problems and to deal with projected cost variances in their early developments.	Cost, budget, deliverables, project status.	
Deficiency Report	Description of an emerging deficiency (work, timing, or budget), including impact analysis and recommended resolution.	Schedule, costs, configuration management, impact analysis.	Candor. Commitment to plan. Management direction.
Earned Value Analysis	Comparison of project completion status to budget expenditure. The regular calculation and analysis of earned value and performance index allows projections of cost variances and schedule slips and serves as an early warning system of project performance problems.	Schedule, budget, deliverables, cost-time tradeoff.	Measurable milestones. Ability to estimate cost and time-to-complete. Trust. Risk sharing. Ownership.
Interface Chart	A chart of N × N elements defining the inputs, outputs, and timing to and from N interfacing work groups. Chart can also be used as part of QFD to define and manage the "customers" of the business process.	Task leaders, cross-functional communications, QFD framework.	Established cross-functional linkages. Management support and leadership.
PERT/CPM	Time-activity network showing task flow, interfaces and dependencies. Used for comprehensive analysis of project schedules and schedule changes.	Schedule, budget, deliverables, cost-time tradeoff.	Accurate cost, time and technical performance data. Measurable milestones.

Table 1 Analytical Management Techniques for Project Control

Continued on next page

Analytical Management Technique	Description	Elements of Control	Conditions for Successful Control
Schedule Compression Analysis	Graphical technique for showing compression of overlapping activities due to slippage of earlier or preceding milestones. Serves as early warning system for runaway schedules and costs.	Milestones, deliverables.	Accurate cost, time and technical performance data. Measurable milestones.
Schedule Tracking	Incremental tracking of activities through time by measuring predefined partial results against plan.	Measurable milestone, deliverables, micro-schedule.	Accurate cost, time and technical performance data.
Simulation	Simulation of a technical, business, or project situation based on some form of a model. Applications range from a simple test to computer-assisted analysis of complex business scenarios.	Advanced results, feasibility, technology transfer.	Relevant input data and appropriate model. Meaningful interpretation.
Status Assessment	Systematic comparison of technical progress with project schedule and budget data. Analysis of status against plan and possible revision of plan, scope, and business strategy.	Valid project plan, review process, earned value, variance analysis.	Accurate cost, time and technical performance data. Measurable milestones.
Variance Analysis	Analysis of causes of cost and schedule variances, cost-at-completion, earned value, percent of project completion and perfromance index. Applied to project status assessment, reporting and control.	Schedule, costs, configuration management, impact analysis, management.	

Table 1—*Continued*

been no universal evidence on the effectiveness of the more contemporary tools (Thamhain 1994b). Further, few guidelines have been published in the literature on how and where to use these new tools and techniques most appropriately. Perhaps one of the greatest challenges for management is to seek management tools and techniques that meet the triple constraint:

- compatible with the business environment, processes, cultures, and values
- conducive to specific problem solving, which usually involves a whole spectrum of factors from innovation to decision-making, cross-functional communications, and dealing with risks and uncertainty
- useful for tracking and controlling the project according to established plans.

Process-Oriented Management Technique	Description	Elements of Control	Conditions for Successful Control
Concurrent Engineering	In-parallel/concurrent execution of project phases; "seamless product development." Objectives: reducing project cost and cycle time, increasing responsiveness to customer/market dynamics. Also, an effective tool for multifunctional integration and technology transfer.	Input-output definition, interface definition, QFD, DFM/A, DICE, rapid prototyping, structured analysis.	Organization interface agreement. Personal commitment. Effective communications and organizational linkages.
Benchmarking	Comparing one system, process or practice to another (usually best-in-class) with the objective to improve performance.	Performance metrics. Business process.	Measurability of comparative metrics. Ability to diagnose/analyze the cause of differences. Ability to adapt tools or methods.
Design Review	Review of the project baseline at various stages of development, such as preliminary, critical or final design review. Objective: examine and predict functionality of the deliverable system early in the project cycle.	Baseline, design parameters, documentation, multifunctional reviewers, agenda.	Multidisciplinary preparation/homework. Presence of all technology transfer agents. Competence and willingness to analyze implementation and transferability.
Out-of-Bounds Review	Critical review and impact assessment of a situation declared as out-of-bounds.	Review, analysis, corrective action plan, visibility, peer pressure, management control.	Mutual trust and respect among team members. Power sharing among managers and with team.
Project Definition	Front-end planning of a project and its resource and timing requirements. Objective: project definition/organization, task delegation, project tracking and control.	Schedule, budget, task roster, task matrix, statement of work, task authorization, resource leveling.	Team involvement. Desire to participate. Risk sharing and power sharing among managers and with team. Senior management involvement and support.
Project Review	Technical and contractual review of project status against established plans.	Professional review, C/SCSC, PERT/CPM, variance analysis.	
Prototyping	Advanced build of a design for the purpose of testing functionality and performance prior to production or deployment.	Design process, simulation, CAD/CAM, project management.	Relevant baseline. Effective prototype testing and evaluation.
Quality Function Deployment (QFD)	TQM concept know as House of Quality. Used for mapping the technology transfer flow throughout an organization and its markets, identifying for each organizational unit: inputs, outputs and specific "internal customer" and their requirements.	Organizational interface and input-output definition, internal and external customer focus.	Team involvement. Desire to participate. Risk sharing and power sharing among managers and with team. Senior management involvement and support.
Requirements Analysis	Distinct project planning phase which defines the specific technical, resource, market and timing requirements for the project baseline. Often coupled with Voice of the Customer and strategic assessment.	Needs assessment, Voice of the Customer, project planning.	
Stage-Gate Process	Phased approach to project planning and management. Defines "gates" for consecutive stages which check the feasibility and provide implementation focus and control.	Phased planning, modular work plan deliverables, check points, sign-offs, gate reviews, process action teams, focus groups, multidisciplinary teams, management.	
Stage-Gate Review	Specific review at the end of a project stage with deliverables and checkpoints, predefined as part of the stage-gate process. Can incorporate other project or design reviews.		
Voice of the Customer	Distinct project planning phase which defines the specific technical, resource, market and timing requirements for the project baseline, with focus on the specific customer needs.	Needs assessment, market analysis, focus group, survey, customer feedback.	

Table 2   Process-Oriented Management Techniques for Project Control

People-Oriented Management Technique	Description	Elements of Control	Conditions for Successful Control
Core Team	A team of resource managers responsible for planning, organization and execution of many projects of a similar nature.	Dedicated functional management team, minimum cross-functional impedance.	Proper team design and charter. Effective communication channels, internal and external. Competent team members and desire to participate. Risk sharing and power sharing among managers and within team. Autonomy. Senior management involvement and support. Effective conflict management system. Team-based evaluations and awards. Minimum fear. Reasonable job security. Managerial checks and balances. Team leadership.
Design/Build	Typically used in product development projects, new team members are integrated into the project team as it moves from the product design to the product build stages, while retaining key members from the earlier project stages.	Shared multifunctional experience, project/team ownership, high technical competence of team.	
Focus Group	A group of "stakeholders" within a project organization or its support functions engaging in self-study and analysis of the project management system or the business process with the objective to improve it.	Problem ownership, pride, personal/professional needs, will change status quo.	
Joint Performance Evaluation	Both project performance and individual performance are defined in terms of end-objectives, hence including multifunctional measures. The objective is to enhance cross-functional cooperation and team integration.	Stakeholder/ownership, mutual dependency, risk sharing, internal customer orientation.	
Self-Directed Team	Individual team members and the project teams as a whole are given high levels of autonomy and accountability (empowerment) toward plan implementation. This forces higher degrees of multidisciplinary decision-making and work integration at the operational level.	Stakeholder/ownership, mutual dependency, risk sharing, internal customer orientation, personal commitment and drive, team communication and decision-making.	

Table 3   People-Oriented Management Techniques for Project Control

The second challenge is for management to implement selected project control tools and techniques into a business process. This involves careful integration of these tools with the various physical, informational, managerial and psychological subsystems of the enterprise to minimize the risk of rejection. The third challenge is for management to create and facilitate a learning process for these tools and techniques to become institutionalized and used by the people in the organization, because they help in getting their projects done more effectively and create visibility and recognition for their work.

In the decades ahead, the ability to effectively manage projects will play a decisive role in separating winning companies from the losers. Largely because of new technology in computers and communications, project management tools and techniques will further proliferate, be fine-tuned, and be applied across a wide range of business situations. The sophistication and effectiveness with which these tools are being applied will profoundly influence the way companies do business, utilize their resources, handle project complexities, achieve quality, and respond to market requirements with speed and accuracy. Technology-based business environments are expected to further amplify both the challenges and the opportunities that lie ahead.

Study Method. The study for this paper began with a literature review and extensive field studies into project management practices conducted between 1993 and 1995 with focus on the concepts, tools, and techniques used for managerial control in technology-based work environments. This initial study formed the basis for a detailed survey design involving a combination of action research and questionnaires. The field study yielded data from sixty-two project teams with a total sample population of 294 professionals: 186 engineers, scientists, and technicians; twenty-three supervisors; thirty-eight project team leaders; eighteen project managers; ten directors of R&D; nine directors of marketing; and ten general management executives. The data received covered over 180 projects, mostly high-technology product/service developments with budgets averaging $1,200,000 each. All project teams saw themselves working in a high-technology environment. The host companies are large technology-based multinational companies of the Fortune 1000 category. Data were collected between 1993 and 1995 by questionnaires and two qualitative methods: participant observation and in-depth retrospective interviewing. The purpose of this combined data collection method was to cast the broadest possible information-gathering net to identify the tools, techniques, and practices used for managing technical projects today and to gain insight into applications, methods, and effectiveness.

CONTROLLING THE PROJECT—ACCORDING TO PLAN

Cultural and philosophical differences obviously influence the way companies manage their projects and set up control systems. Even within one department, methods may differ from project to project. However, this study shows that general agreement seems to exist among project leaders on the type of tools and techniques that find general application in today's technology-based project environments. Using content analysis of the survey data, management-control techniques were identified and organized into three primary categories, focusing on analytical, procedural, and people-oriented tools and techniques, as summarized in Tables 1, 2 and 3.

Analytical Tools and Techniques. Effective project management involves a great variety of analytical tools and methods. Many of these tools, such as critical path analysis and budget tracking, have been around for a long time. But, in recent years, they have been redefined to more appropriately fit contemporary challenges and be more conducive to today's business environment, which includes self-directed teams, cross-functional alliances, and the need for flexible and speedy implementation. Further, 92 percent of the analytical applications have been enhanced with the integration of sophisticated computer software.

We find specifically that analytical tools must be congruent with the business process and the human factors of project management to work effectively. That is, analytical techniques work only if (1) the inputs, such as time and resource estimates, percent complete, and skill levels are accurate, and (2) the people responsible for implementation will use these tools and analytical results to correct problems and deficiencies in the plan. A prerequisite is the team members' mutual trust, respect, candor, and the ability to fail-safe and thus share risks. Equally important, the work environment must foster effective communications, cross-functional linkages, and a business process conducive to interconnecting people, activities, and support functions. Therefore, it is not surprising to find that successful application of these analytical tools depends predominately upon human factors:

- personal commitment to project results
- management involvement and support
- effective cross-functional communications
- mutual trust and respect among team members
- risk sharing and fail-safe conditions
- motivation and direction toward results
- managerial leadership.

Process-Oriented Tools and Techniques. Most of the emerging tools focus on the management process for project control (Jackman 1989/1990; Rigby 1995). They often represent a true innovation of the business process; they at least represent an extension of established business processes. Examples are concurrent engineering (Thamhain 1994a), stage-gate processes, and quality function deployment (Thamhain 1996a). Similar to analytical techniques, process-oriented management concepts also rely heavily on human factors. However, in contrast to analytical tools, process-oriented tools cannot merely be handed to the team or be used selectively; they must be carefully integrated with the project management system and its processes. Taken together, successful application of process-oriented tools and techniques requires understanding of management tools and applications; management support; clear statement of objectives and their significance; project team ownership in control techniques; controls integrated with project management process; controls integrated with the human-resource system and personal rewards; effective cross-functional communications; managers who share power and control with project team; and competent, motivated project team with ownership to the project objectives.

People-Oriented Tools and Techniques. Effective project management involves a whole spectrum of people issues:

- clear direction and guidance
- ability to plan and elicit commitments
- communication skills
- assistance in problem solving
- ability to deal effectively with managers and support personnel across functional lines, often with little or no formal authority
- information-processing skills
- ability to collect and filter relevant data valid for decision-making in a dynamic environment
- ability to integrate individual demands, requirements, and limitations into decisions that benefit the overall project.

It further involves the project manager's ability to resolve intergroup conflicts and to build multifunctional teams. These findings, further supported by other research (Thamhain and Wilemon 1996), consistently emphasize the important role of organizational and cultural factors. These factors involve the human side of project control, complicating the otherwise analytically and procedurally straightforward processes. In response to these challenges, an increasing number of companies are capitalizing on people as one of the most critical elements in the managerial control system. These companies realize that successful application of these people-oriented tools and techniques requires project teams involved in tool development and setup; mutual trust and respect by team and management; provisions to deal with emerging conflicts; process integration with functional support groups; senior management support; concepts, tools, and techniques integrated with the human resource system; effective cross-functional communications; managers who share power and control with project team; competent, motivated project teams with ownership to the project objectives; project team structure conducive to using tools and techniques; and people who can work in unstructured environments.

SATISFACTION WITH PROJECT MANAGEMENT TECHNIQUES

One wonders why managerial tools, designed to improve project performance and highly recommended for their effectiveness, have not been more widely adopted. Popularity of a particular control technique in the management literature and actual applications to project situations are two different things. Few companies go into a major restructuring of their business processes lightly. At best, the introduction of a new project-control technique is painful, costly, and disruptive to ongoing operations. At worst, it can destroy existing managerial controls and can lead to mistrust among team members and management, game playing, power struggles, conflict, and misleading information. It also can lead to a transfer of accountability and action-orientation away from team members and project leaders and to the control-tool mechanics. In fact, the risks of introducing a new project-control tool are so substantial that many managers are willing to live with an inefficient system rather than go through the trouble of changing it. Most skeptical are managers who have tried a specific tool and obtained disappointing results or outright failures. These negative impressions are often most intensive for complex process-oriented controls such as stage-gate techniques, which rely on complex and often fuzzy measures of performance. Typical reasons for rejecting or underutilizing project controls are summarized in Table 4; the listing is rank-ordered by frequency as given by project leaders. Table 4 summarizes specifically the responses to our survey question, "Why are the tools and techniques, used in your organization for project control, underused or rejected?" (This question was a follow-on to a series of questions probing into the types and effectiveness of control tools and techniques in use at a particular organization. Questionnaires and interviews were used to collect the data. The 1,350 responses were summarized into the composite shown in Table 4.) Although these resource managers, project leaders, and team members responded differently as to the type of reason, frequency, and situational impact, they were statistically not significant enough to separate these populations. In fact, agreement among the three populations was verified at a 95 percent confidence level (using a Kruskal-Wallis analysis of variance by ranks), indicating that the concerns and reasons for underusing or rejecting these tools are shared across different levels of managerial responsibility.

The reasons for underusing or rejecting project controls can be divided into four classes:

1. Lack of confidence that tools will produce benefits.
2. Anxieties over potentially harmful side effects.
3. Conflict among users over the method or results.
4. Method too difficult and burdensome, or it interferes with the work process.

Interestingly, most of the perceived problems are based on *feelings* and *assumptions* rather than on specific measures, comparisons, and analytical facts. Only about 20 percent of the reasons given could be supported with examples from personal experience. This suggests a potentially negative bias toward new and untried tools and techniques. Of course, basic psychology tells us that this behavior is quite normal and should be anticipated. Management must recognize the potential barriers toward project-control tools, which might result from anxieties, misunderstandings, unpleasant experiences, or other unfavorable perceptions. Management must deal with these perceptions and develop a positive attitude among project team members toward these new tools to avoid rejection before a fair evaluation is made of their usability and value. Specifically, the findings emphasize the importance of behavioral variables: good leadership, personal interest and commitment to the project, potential for recognition, management interest, and perceived project importance and priority. All have favorable correlation to the team members' willingness to accept and proactively work with project controls.

RECOMMENDATIONS FOR USING PROJECT MANAGEMENT CONTROLS EFFECTIVELY

Pressures for improving business performance, combined with the emergence of new tools and techniques that promise more effective project control, have prompted management to cautiously explore the relevancy of these new concepts. So far, management focus has

Why Project Management Tools and Techniques Are Underused or Rejected?

[Typical reasons listed in decreasing order of frequency perceived by project leaders.]

1. Lack of understanding on how to use tools properly.
2. General anxiety over methods and information use and misuse.
3. Use of tool requires too much work, is too time-consuming, and requires too much paperwork.
4. Tools reduce personal drive and willingness to fix ad hoc problems and contingencies.
5. Not consistent with already established project management procedures and business processes.
6. Control method is threatening, regarding performance assessment, personal freedom, or autonomy.
7. Conflicting points of view among team members regarding the tool value or appropriate use.
8. *Not-invented-here* syndrome.
9. Conflict among managers or project team members about value of tool or application method.
10. Cost of acquisition and implementation is too high.
11. Tools focus on project management metrics, neglecting the importance of teamwork and cooperation.
12. Unclear purpose, objective, benefit, and value.
13. Tool leads to unwanted additional policies and procedures.
14. Too busy to learn new tool or technique.
15. Uncomfortable with new or unfamiliar methods.
16. Disagreement over application method or use of data.
17. Tools don't help in control, but help to maintain status quo when project performance deteriorates.
18. Stifles multifunctional communications and complex decision-making.
19. Reduces face-to-face communications and multidisciplinary problem solving.
20. Stifles technical innovation and search for solutions to complex problems.
21. Tools are seen as substitute for management support and decision-making.
22. Tools isolate team members and their leaders.
23. Prior bad experience with tool or technique.
24. Tools weaken managerial power.
25. Not consistent with self-directed team concept.

Table 4 Perception on Project Management Techniques

been predominantly on the operational process of project management and its traditional schedule/budget performance measures. In its aim to improve operational performance, management often overlooks three important aspects of the project management process and its overall performance. First, tools and techniques are seldom integrated with the business process. Second, the impact on intrinsic project performance is rarely being considered; that is, the impact of a new process on innovation, creativity, quality, customer relations, and the ability to cope with changing requirements is rarely evaluated and factored into designing and fine-tuning new controls. Third, the human side of organizational change is often poorly managed or outright ignored. Introducing new managerial controls, as minor as a new weekly review procedure or as massive as changing to concurrent engineering, involves organizational change. It is associated with hopes, fears, anxieties, likes, and dislikes, plus a good dose of organizational politics. One of the strongest messages from this study points to the fact that people are still the most vital part of any managerial control system. A new system at least has a chance for consideration if the project team believes in the value of the tool to make its job easier and more effective—to help produce desired results, visibility, and recognition while minimizing anxieties and fears over administrative burdens, restrictions of freedom and autonomy, and any negative impact on personal growth and security. Few companies have attacked these softer, more subtle issues of project control and tool implementation, which are crucial for overall business performance, especially in technology-based environments. These issues often need special attention and resources to ensure the effective integration of these tools into the business process and their effective use by project team members.

A number of recommendations for effectively implementing and using managerial controls for technical projects have been derived from the field study. These recommendations should help both project leaders and their managers to understand the complex interaction of organizational and behavioral variables that affect implementing appropriate managerial tools and techniques to control technology-based projects. These findings should increase the awareness of what works and what doesn't and help project management fine-tune control systems toward high performance. The findings should also help scholars to better understand the complexities involved in controlling project management processes and to use this study as a building block for further research.

Involve the Team. Make your people part of the selection and implementation process. Both the project team and the project manager should be involved in assessing the project situation and evaluating new control tools. Critical factor analysis, focus groups, and process action teams are good vehicles for team involvement and collective decision-making, which lead to ownership, greater acceptance of the selected tool, and willingness for continuous improvement and effective use.

Make Tools Consistent with the Work Process. Management controls should be an integral part of the business process. Particular attention should be paid to the workability of the tools and techniques for integrating tasks and transferring technology across organizational lines.

Build on Existing Tools and Systems. The highest levels of acceptance and successful application of management tools are found in areas where new tools are added incrementally to already existing management-control systems. These situations should be identified and addressed first.

Use Established Management Practices. Radically new methods are usually greeted with great anxiety and suspicion. If at all possible, new management tools and techniques should be consistent with established project management practices within an organization. For example, an organization implementing a stage-gate process should make an effort to integrate into the new process already established and proven procedures for project definition, documentation, status reports, reviews, and signoffs. This will make the new management process scan more evolutionary rather than radical. If done correctly, management can use the existing project management system to build upon and incrementally enhance and test new managerial tools and techniques.

Make Tools User Friendly. New project management tools or techniques are more likely to be accepted if they are easy to use and will produce results that are helpful to the users and their work, which includes the organization's senior management.

Anticipate Anxieties and Conflicts. When introducing new tools and techniques, project leaders should anticipate anxieties and conflict among their team members. These negative biases come from uncertainties associated with new working conditions and requirements. They range from personal discomfort with skill requirements to anxieties over the tool's impact on the work process and personal-performance evaluation. These problems should be anticipated and dealt with in a straightforward manner as early as possible.

Ensure No Threat. Management must foster a project team environment of mutual trust and cooperation, an environment that is low on personal conflict, power struggles, surprises, unrealistic demands, and threats to personal and professional integrity. Cooperation with a new (or existing) tool or technique, and commitment to it, can be expected only if its use is relatively risk-free to the user. Unnecessary references to performance appraisals, tight supervision, reduced personal freedom and autonomy, and overhead requirements should be avoided and any concerns dealt with promptly on a personal level.

Foster Challenging Work Environment. Professionally interesting and stimulating work appears to be one of the strongest drivers toward desired results. Verified by several field studies (Deschamps and Nayak 1995; Thamhain 1990; 1996b), we consistently find that the degree of interest and excitement derived from work is directly related to personal effort, the level of team involvement, cross-functional communications, commitment toward established plans, and creativity. Work challenges also produce higher levels of cooperation and some tolerance for risk and conflict. Taken together, work challenge seems to foster a desired behavior conducive to exploring new methods and innovatively applying them to project situations. Further, people who are strongly engaged with their work have a more positive attitude toward change (Thamhain 1989; Thamhain and Wilemon 1996). Therefore, work challenge seems to be a catalyst for integrating team members' personal goals with project objectives and organizational goals. This fosters a favorable climate toward the acceptance and effective use of managerial controls. Project leaders should try to accommodate the professional interests and desires of their personnel whenever possible. One of the best ways to ensure that the work is interesting to team members is to match carefully their personal interests with the scope and needs of the tasks when *signing on* team personnel. In addition, managers should build a project image of importance and high visibility, which can elevate the desirability for participation and contribution.

Pre-Test New Tools and Techniques. Preferably, a new concept should first be tried with a small project and an experienced, high-performance project team. Asking such a team to test, evaluate, and fine-tune the new tool for the company is often seen as an honor and a professional challenge. Further, it usually starts the implementation with a positive attitude and can create an environment of open communications and candor.

Continuous Improvement. Project management tools and techniques are part of the continuously changing business process. Provisions must be made for updating and fine-tuning these tools on an ongoing basis to ensure relevancy to today's project management challenges.

Senior Management Support. Management tools require top-down support to succeed. Through its involvement and communications, management can stress the importance of these tools to the organization, span organizational and cultural boundaries, and unify objectives.

Ensure Proper Direction and Leadership. Throughout the implementation phase of a new management tool or technique, managers can influence the attitude and commitment of their people toward a new concept by their own actions. Concern for project team members, assistance with the use of the tool, and enthusiasm for the project and its administrative-support systems can foster a climate of high motivation, involvement with the project and its management, open communication, and a willingness to cooperate with the new requirements and use them effectively.

A Final Note

The effective implementation and use of project management control tools and techniques can critically determine the success of any project, especially for technology-based undertakings. Successful application of these management controls involves a complex set of variables. The tools must be consistent with the work process and be an integral part of the existing managerial control and personal-reward system. Most importantly, managers must pay attention to human factors. To enhance cooperation with the evaluation, implementation, and effective use of project management controls, project leaders must foster a work environment where people find the controls useful or at least not threatening or interfering with the work process. Further, professionally stimulating work, refueled by visibility and recognition, is conducive to change and cooperation. A professionally stimulating environment seems to lower anxieties over managerial controls, reduce communication barriers and conflict, and enhance the desire of personnel to cooperate and to succeed. It also seems to enhance organizational awareness of the surrounding business environment and the ability to prepare and respond to these challenges effectively by using modern project management techniques. The effective use of modern project-control techniques requires administrative skills for planning and defining project efforts properly and realistically and then tracking the project through its life cycle. Effective project leaders are social architects who understand the interaction of organizational and behavioral variables and can foster a climate of active participation with minimal dysfunctional conflict. They also build alliances with support organizations and upper management to assure organizational visibility, priority, resource availability, and overall support for the multifunctional activities of the project throughout its life cycle.

References

Abdel-Hamid, Tarrek K., and Stuart E. Madnick. 1990. The Elusive Silver Lining: How We Fail to Learn from Software Development Failures. *Sloan Management Review* 32.1: 39–48.

Adler, Paul S., D. William McDonald, and Fred MacDonald. 1992. Strategic Management of Strategic Functions. *Sloan Management Review* 33.2: 19–37.

Anbari, Frank T. 1985. A Systems Approach to Project Evaluation. *Project Management Journal* (Aug.): 21–26.

Archibald, Russell D. 1992. *Managing High-Technology Programs and Projects*. New York: Wiley.

Bahrami, Homa. 1992. The Emerging Flexible Organization: Perspectives from Silicon Valley. *California Management Review* 34.4: 33–52.

Beacon, Glen, et al. 1994. Managing Product Definition in High-Technology Industries: A Pilot Study. *California Management Review* 36.3: 32–56.

Berman, Evan, and Eduardo Vasconcellos. 1994. The Future of Technology Management. *Organization Dynamics* (Winter), and *IEEE Engineering Management Review* 22.3 (Fall): 13–19.

Cash, Charles H., and Robert Fox. 1992. Elements of Successful Project Management. *Project Management Journal* 23.2: 43–47.

Cespedes, Frank. 1994. Industrial Marketing: Managing New Require-ments. *Sloan Management Review* 35.3: 45–60.

Christensen, David S. 1994. A Review of the Cost/Schedule Control Sys-tems Criteria Literature. *Project Management Journal* 25.3 (Sept.): 32–39.

Clark, Kim B., and Steven C. Wheelwright. 1992a. Creating Product Plans to Focus Product Development. *Harvard Business Review* 70.2: 70–82.

———. 1992b. Organizing and Leading Heavyweight Development Teams. *California Management Review* 34.3: 9–28.

Cleland, David I. 1985. A Strategy for Ongoing Project Evaluation. *Project Management Journal* (Aug.): 11–17.

Cunningham, Michael J. 1994. Project Controls: A Practical Approach. *Cost Engineering [ACO]* 36.7: 27–30.

Davies, John R. 1994. Examining the Project Management Process. *Plant Engineering (PLG)* 48: 73–74.

Dean, Burten, et al. 1992. Multiproject Staff Schedule with Variable Resource Constraints. *IEEE Transactions on Engineering Management* 39.1: 59–72.

DeMaio, Adriano, et al. 1994. A Multi-Project Management Framework for New Product Development. *European Journal of Operational Manage-ment* 78.2: 178–91.

Deschamps, Jean-Philippe, and P. Ranganath Nayak. 1995. Implementing World-Class Process. In *Product Juggernauts*. Cambridge: Harvard Press.

Drigani, F. 1989. *Computerized Project Control*. New York: Marcel Dekker.

Gobeli, David H., and Daniel J. Brown. 1993. Improving the Process of Product Innovation. *Research-Technology Management* 32.2: 38–44.

Greiner, Larry E., and Virginia E. Schein. 1981. The Paradox of Managing a Project-Oriented Matrix. *Sloan Management Review* 22.2: 22.

Hatfield, Michael A. 1995. Managing to the Corner Cube: Three-Dimen-sional Management in a Three-Dimensional World. *Project Manage-ment Journal* 26.1: 13–20.

Higgins, J. C., and K. M. Watts. 1986. Some Perspectives on the Use of Man-agement Science Techniques in R&D Management. *R&D Management (UK)* 16.4: 291–96.

Hofman, J. Deborah, and John F. Rockart. 1992. Systems Delivery: Evolving New Strategies. *Sloan Management Review* 33.4: 21–31.

———. 1994. Application Templates: Faster, Better and Cheaper systems. *Sloan Management Review* 36.1: 49–60.

Jackman, Hal. 1989/1990. State-of-the-Art Project Management Method-ologies: A Survey. *Optimum* 20.4: 24–47.

Kernaghan, J. A. 1986. The Contribution of the Group Process to Successful Project Planning in R&D. *IEEE Transactions on Engineering Manage-ment* 33.3: 134–40.

Knutson, Joan. 1996. A Socio-Technical Model of Project Management. *PM Network* 10.8: 5–7.

Larson, Erik W., & David H. Gobeli. 1987. Matrix Management: Contradictions and Insight. *California Management Review* 29.4: 126–38.

Lewis, James P. 1991. *Project Planning, Scheduling and Control.* Probus.

Lovitt, Mike. 1996. Continuous Improvement through the QS-9000 Roadmap. *Quality Progress* 29.2: 39–43.

Manganelli, Raymond L., and Mark M. Klein. (1994). Your Reengineering Toolkit. *Management Review* 83: 26–30.

Martinez, Erwin V. 1995. Successful Reengineering Demands IS/Business Partnerships. *Sloan Management Review* 36.4: 51–60.

Mintzberg, Henry. 1994. Rounding out the Manager's Job. *Sloan Management Review* 36.1: 11–26.

Moder, Joseph J. 1994. Conjecture on the Future Direction of MPM. *Project Management Journal* 25.3: 6–7.

1995 Project Management Software Survey. 1995. *PM Network* 9.7: 35–44.

Oberlender, Garold D., and W. William Abel. 1995. Project Management Improves Well Control Event. *Oil & Gas Journal* 93.28: 56–63.

Prasad, Biren. 1995. A Structured Approach to Product and Process Optimization. *International Journal of Quality and Reliability Management* 12.9: 123–38.

Ramping up (editorial). 1995. *Midrange Systems* 8.21: 23–24.

Randolph, W. Alan, and Barry Z. Posner. 1988. What Every Manager Needs to Know about Project Management. *Sloan Management Review* 29.4: 65–73.

Raz, Tzvi. 1993. Introduction of the Project Management Discipline in a Software Development Organization. *IBM Systems Journal* 32.2: 265–77.

Rigby, Darrel K. 1995. Managing the Management Tools. *Engineering Management Review* 23.1: 88–92.

Roberts, Tom L., Jr., and Carry T. Hughes. 1996. Obstacles to Implementing a System Development Methodology. *Journal of Systems Management* 47.2: 36–40.

Slevin, Dennis P., and Jeffrey K. Pinto. 1987. Balancing Strategy and Tactics in Project Implementation. *Sloan Management Review* 29.1: 33–41.

Sprague, David A., and Randy Greenwell. 1992. Project Management: Are Employees Trained to Work in Project Teams? *Project Management Journal* 23.1: 22–26.

Thamhain, Hans J. 1989. Validating Project Plans. *Project Management Journal* 20.4.

———. 1990. Managing Technologically Innovative Team Efforts toward New Product Success. *Project Management Journal* 7.1.

———. 1994a. A Manager's Guide to Effective Concurrent Project Management. *PM Network* 8.11: 6–10.

———. 1994b. Designing Project Management Systems for a Radically Changing World. *Project Management Journal* 25.4: 6–7.

———. 1996a. Applying Stage-Gate Reviews to Accelerated Product Developments. *Proceedings of PMI '96 Annual Symposium of the Project Management Institute*, October 4–10.

———. 1996b. Managing Technology-Based Innovation. In *Handbook of Technology Management*, G. Gayner, ed. New York: McGraw-Hill.

Thamhain, Hans J., and Joseph Weiss. 1992. Project Management Methods: Strategic and Competitive Uses in High-Technology Companies. *Engineering Management Journal* 4.4.

Thamhain, Hans J., and David L. Wilemon. 1986. Criteria for Controlling Projects According to Plan. *Project Management Journal*: 75–81.

———. (1996). Building High-Performing Engineering Project Teams. In *The Human Side of Managing Technological Innovation*, R. Katz, ed. Oxford Press.

Thomasen, Ole B., and Leslie Butterfield. 1993. Combining Risk Management and Resource Optimization in Project Management Software. *Cost Engineering* 35.8: 19–24.

Tippett, Donald D., and David A. Waits. 1994. Project Management and TQM: Why Aren't Project Managers Coming on Board? *Industrial Management* 36: 12–15.

Program Control from the Bottom Up—Exploring the Working Side

Raymond K. Johnson, Battelle, Pacific Northwest Laboratory

Project Management Journal (March 1985)

PROGRAM CONTROL IS a business comprised of many systems and techniques. All businesses must have some kind of program control system. Many large corporations, especially those dealing with the United States government, employ elaborate and complex program control systems with which to monitor program activity and measure program progress and performance. These systems provide information to management for the decision-making processes.

Many publications deal with theory and the mechanics of implementation, execution, and performance. This approach may be termed *looking at program control from the top down*. The reverse of that perspective addresses the subject from the *bottom up*. At Battelle-Northwest, the personnel charged with the development, implementation, and maintenance of program-control systems for research programs are known as management information and support specialists or program control specialists.

At Battelle-Northwest, the program-control specialist encounters people with widely different academic and experience backgrounds. For instance, personnel at the Pacific Northwest Laboratory include geologists, biologists, nuclear scientists, psychologists, engineers, financial and administrative specialists, mathematicians, hydrologists, and many other disciplines too numerous to mention. Also included are support personnel such as contract administrators, personnel specialists, craftsmen, and so forth. A high percentage of the personnel have advanced degrees, including over three hundred Ph.D's. The program-control specialist's challenge is to develop beneficial program control systems while dealing with personnel who have diverse backgrounds.

Some approaches, techniques, obstacles, and problems that confront the program-control specialist in his everyday work are presented here. Some possible solutions to the obstacles are discussed. Here, the working side of program control from the viewpoint of the personnel functioning in this field is explored. Also discussed are some of the characteristics that go into the making of an effective program-control specialist.

BACKGROUND

About six years ago, Battelle-Northwest made a decision to develop the research project management system for projects over $100,000. After about three years of development effort, which included two years of general application, internal reviews at that time indicated that progress had been as good as hoped (Patrick 1979). Since then, Battelle has established a department dedicated entirely to management information and support, which includes program-control activities. In 1978, a program-control system was developed and implemented for the Department of Energy's fuels refabrication and development (FRAD) program. The goal of the FRAD program was to develop a spent-nuclear-fuels refabrication technology base for proliferation-resistant fuel cycles to a point when the choice of desirable fuel cycles would not be limited by refabrication technology. Included in the program plan were the design, construction, and operation of a remote fuels refabrication laboratory. The original plan called for the expenditure of $178,000,000. The FRAD program achieved a high level of success, and the Department of Energy rated the overall performance *excellent*. It is believed that the utilization of the program-control system contributed substantially toward the award of that excellent rating.

Another Battelle-Northwest program, the seasonal thermal energy storage (STES) program, also received an *excellent* rating from the Department of Energy. Its objective is to demonstrate the economic storage and retrieval of energy on a seasonal basis. It uses heat or cold available from waste sources or other sources during a surplus period to reduce peak period demand, reduce electric utilities' peaking problems, and contribute to the establishment of favorable economics for district heating and cooling systems. Aquifers, ponds, earth, and lakes have potential for seasonal storage. The program-control system developed for the STES program contributed toward its excellent rating.

THE PROGRAM CONTROL SPECIALIST

Many papers, articles, and books published on the subject of program control are oriented toward managers who need a program-control system or to the person charged with the responsibility of having the system maintained. These articles dwell essentially on theory and the mechanics of implementation, execution, and performance. This could be referred to as looking at the subject from the *top down*. Why top down? The system is designed to provide information to the manager for decision-making processes. The manager is the user; the manager is the one who benefits from the use of the system; the manager is the one at the top.

It is interesting to take a look at program-control systems from the viewpoint of the personnel charged with the development, implementation, and maintenance of the system. At Battelle-Northwest, a division of Battelle Memorial Institute, the largest contract-research organization in the world, the program-control specialist has responsibility for this activity.

Technical aspects of program control, or the advantages of one technique or system versus another, will not be addressed. Rather, what could be called the *working side of program control* is discussed. In exploring this level of program management, many questions arise. Following are a few of them.

- What kind of person is best suited to this type of work?
- Is one temperament more than any other likely to adapt to this endeavor?
- Is personality a major factor of successful accomplishment in this area?
- What are the requisites for a program-control specialist?

31

The answers to the first three questions are difficult and better left to professionals qualified in human behavior. The answer to the fourth question is complex and not necessarily precise. The attempt here is to convey some of the approaches and techniques that can be used in program control, together with possible solutions to obstacles and problems that confront the program-control specialist in her everyday work.

The ultimate goal of program control is to ensure a quality product on schedule and within cost. A program-control specialist in some research development environments has to deal with budgets, schedules, and people. The program-control specialist must not only have a good understanding of program control systems but also must be able to set and enforce deadlines for data input without formal authority, overcome resistance when it emerges, and yet maintain a good working relationship with her fellow workers. The people with whom she deals have widely differing academic and experience backgrounds that may require her to use subtle variations in conduct. Many research managers may advocate management approaches for the achievement of goals that are inconsistent with accepted program-control procedures and techniques for the accomplishment of those same goals. Many research managers have had little or no previous experience with systemized program control and may be reluctant to accept assistance in this area. *Herein lies the challenge for the program control specialist.*

CONTROLS

In some organizations, the use of program-control systems is dictated as mandatory by upper management or by the customer—i.e., the Department of Defense (1976, 1977). The Department of Energy also identifies some projects for implementation of full or modified cost/schedule control-system criteria (1979). This is not universally true of either department, however—especially in research and development.

Every endeavor needs to consider and approach cost/schedule control in order to maintain visibility. With a good system in place, chances of cost overruns and missed scheduled milestones are reduced.

The author's experience has been only with research and development programs, so only those types of programs are addressed.

To implement a program-control system, it must be recognized that the dollar amount and scope of the program should dictate the complexity of the control system to be used. Care must be taken to not *overcontrol*. To not overcontrol means that care must be taken, when establishing control thresholds, not to apply thresholds that are too stringent. The dictionary defines *threshold* as 1) same as doorsill; 2) the entrance or beginning point of something (at the threshold of a new career); and, 3) the point at which a stimulus is just enough to be perceived or produce a response (the threshold of pain). In program control, threshold means the point at which variance analyses must be provided, when the dollar expenditures exceed the predetermined allowance for above or below the budgeted dollars. Although overcontrol may cause problems, *undercontrol* also may cause problems. Undercontrol connotes that control thresholds that are too lax can lead to *no control*. In other words, keep the complexity or size of the program-control system commensurate with the complexity of the program. The smaller the dollar volume of a program, the less elaborate the control system need be.

Forms used in the control system should be designed so that they are concise, simple, and not *too busy*. Complicated forms can aggravate personnel, sometimes to the point where individuals become uncooperative. Most people can relate to this when they consider the 1040 form used for federal income tax purposes. A form's design should include space for all necessary information, and no more. A pitfall to be avoided is adding little boxes or lines for information that is *nice to have*. If it is not necessary, it should not be included. In some cases, it may be necessary to divide one form into two forms. Signature lines should be held only to those required by the administrative system in use. Sometimes, the documents' reviewers may initial it prior to final signature rather than using an excessive number of signature lines. Complicated forms can create resistance or fear, which makes the program-control specialist's job more difficult.

There are those who are of the opinion that research and development programs cannot be scheduled and budgeted in the same manner as production programs. Experience indicates that this may not be true in all cases. For example, the Department of Defense—the Air Force, to be specific—employs cost/schedule control-system criteria on major systems acquisitions, many of which are research and development procurements. An example is the B-1 program conducted by Rockwell International in Los Angeles, California, in the

United States. The Air Force criteria can also be used on smaller programs. In November 1980, the Air Force issued a pamphlet, ASD-173-2, Implementation Guide of Cost/Status Reporting of Low Dollar Value R&D Contracts. The modified criteria are sometimes referred to as the mini-mini-PMS. When applying the modified criteria, as indicated previously, care must be taken to not apply excessively restrictive thresholds that may overcontrol.

TECHNIQUE

Try to imagine yourself in the place of a program-control specialist who has been assigned the task of implementing a program-control system on a new program that is funded on a larger scale than the program manager has administered in the past. Also, assume this manager has never been exposed to structured, disciplined program control.

The first item of business for the specialist is to meet with the program manager and management team, if known at that time, to establish the general outline of the system to be used. The conversation will probably be a give-and-take discussion, as this program manager is not acquainted with systemized program control. The philosophy of program control should be discussed, after which detailed explanations and suggestions will be offered. The first meeting is of utmost importance! This is when the program-control specialist has an opportunity to begin to establish credibility. His first chance to gain the confidence of the manager to whom he will provide support may be won or lost at that time. The meeting will be a combination of education for the manager and an exercise in tact, diplomacy, and persuasion for the program-control specialist.

As an example of the kind of situation that could confront the program-control specialist, put yourself in his place. Imagine what your reaction would be if, at the outset, the manager said: "Do we really need a program control system? I've been doing research here for a good many years without such a system, and I've managed to survive." Merely surviving is not enough. To remain healthy and grow in business, the firm must excel in product quality, keep costs competitive, and maintain schedule integrity. A good control system can significantly and cost-effectively contribute to those goals. This situation could challenge the persuasive talents of the specialist. This is an opportunity to extol the benefits and advantages of program control; the specialist must present a convincing case.

RESISTANCE

Most articles concerning program control do not comment on how to cope with or react to the aforementioned kinds of resistance situations. Resistance situations require considerable thought and subtlety to overcome seemingly natural resistance. When confronted with a question of need for a program control system, the program-control specialist might answer the question as follows:

> This particular program has a bigger dollar volume than your past programs and has specific goals to be achieved. It is important to have the costs planned and work scheduled as soon a s possible. In other words, we must plan, so the work will be completed to meet the sponsor's schedule. Also, as changes occur—which they will—we will be able to more quickly recognize them and adjust accordingly.

It would be appropriate at this time to suggest that an outline of the program-control system be prepared and then later discussed and finalized. An example of a simple but effective program-control system could be one that is developed using a work breakdown structure, cost plan by month, trend curves, milestone logs, detail schedules, summary logic network, master schedule, and a monthly report containing a technical progress narrative and displaying cost/schedule status with a variance analysis that explains cost/schedule variances. Bringing this manager around may require time, patience, and perseverance to educate him to the advantages of program control.

NO RESISTANCE

The program-control specialist will not always be confronted with resistance when installing systems. She may be assigned to support a program manager who is an advocate of systemized program control. This type of manager may want to plan her program at too fine a level, which can be just as dangerous as not planning in sufficient detail. In this case, it should be pointed out that finite control or micromanagement has its disadvantages and can create too much paperwork. It could require excessive man-hours for tracking, updating schedules, and preparing reports. The *advocate* manager may set the variance thresholds too tightly. Variance thresholds that are too stringent can create excessive and somewhat useless variance reports, required to explain insignificant variations from the plan. Too-restrictive tolerance bands can be characterized as overcontrolling. Trying to control at too low a level of the work breakdown structure can also be described as overcontrolling.

WORK BREAKDOWN STRUCTURE

The three words—*work, breakdown,* and *structure*—when defined separately are found to have more than one meaning. Definitions found in the dictionary for each of the three words include the single meaning:

- work: labor, toil
- breakdown: a separation into parts
- structure: the arrangement or interrelation of all of the parts for a whole.

The Department of Energy defines a work breakdown structure as "a product-oriented family tree division of hardware, software, facilities, and other items, which organizes, defines, and displays all of the work to be performed in accomplishing the project objectives" (1980).

One of the first steps in the development of a program-control system for a program is to develop a work breakdown structure. When preparing it, one of three things can occur:

- not enough detail
- too much detail
- the right amount of detail.

Discussing the work breakdown structure with the task leaders during its preparation is a must and may require tact. It is appropriate to remember that each person is different, and situations will vary according to the individual. Some task leaders may tell you that they need only plan for one task—for example, synthetic fuels toxicity studies (not enough detail). The next level of resistance that may be encountered is here. The program-control specialist's persuasive talent can significantly influence the program planning. For example, the task leader who has responsibility for synthetic fuels toxicity studies has proposed that this is a single task; therefore, there is no need to divide the work into smaller segments. Also, for example, the task leader has defined ten individual studies and must perform the studies utilizing the efforts of four other researchers. At this point, the knowledgeable program-control specialist will see trouble looming in the future. From the accounting standpoint, all costs will be collected into a common account. The task leader will be unable to track the cost of each test being conducted for each study. If one (or more) study gets into trouble costwise, it will not be apparent because the costs for all of the tests are *lumped* together. This could put the task leader into an overrun condition later in the project. Some studies may have to be scaled down or deleted as a result of the undetected cost overrun of the offending studies.

By breaking the work into smaller pieces, better and more detailed planning can take place. Also, the costs for each element can be tracked. Detailed schedules prepared for the smaller segments can be monitored, thereby affording the task leader early identification of potential or real problems. This will better enable the task leader to consider alternatives and make decisions for corrective measures before irreversible damage becomes manifest.

It is within the province of the program-control specialist to demonstrate to the task leader that it is important to break the work down into a controllable or manageable level. The program-control specialist should encourage the synthetic fuels toxicity studies task leader to break the study into substudies for various synthetic fuels. Were those substudies broken down further into various tests performed on each fuel, it might be too much detail. The detail to which the work should be broken down is a matter of judgment, oftentimes based on experience, that should be discussed and negotiated with the task leader.

One of the most significant advantages of program control is that in order to implement a control system, the program/project manager/task leader must actively engage in a planning exercise. She must plan her portion of the program! To the program and the program manager, this planning is important. The program-control system forces her to plan.

It is also important to understand that after the plan is developed, it should be *statused* at regular intervals—usually every month. Also, the manager should be careful to keep the plan meaningful. In other words, if the plan become unrealistic, a replanning exercise should take place to realign the program-planning document with the current situation. The manager should never report to a plan that has become invalid.

Data Collection

The installation of a program-control system includes formulation of a work plan from which the program progress and performance can be measured from cost and schedule standpoints. Data must be gathered from the task leaders or those who will actually do the work. This data will consist of a task statement(s) and estimates of man-hours, travel expenses, capital equipment costs, special test-equipment costs, materials, and so forth required for performing the work. At this time, milestones will also be identified for schedule preparation.

When developing schedules, care should be taken to identify milestones and activities that recognize significant constraints and relationships. Milestones should be objectively measurable. The schedule hierarchy should contain a summary or master schedule and related subordinate schedules that provide a logical sequence from the contract level to the lowest-level work breakdown structure element. The program manager should emphasize to the task leaders that the identification of milestones will not be used against them. He should stress that when milestone dates are unachievable, replanning is in order.

At this point, problems may be encountered. As each task leader is an individual, it must be recognized that techniques required for eliciting information from these uniquely different people may vary. Some technical people are reluctant to supply information. The reasons are many, but the one that stands out is that they believe that information relating to a schedule will tie them to specific dates and cost regimens that may not allow them flexibility in their work. Also, if these researchers have not been subject to the discipline of program control, they may resent invasion into their territory. It makes them nervous. It is extremely important for the program-control specialist to have the program manager's confidence. With faith in the program-control specialist, the task leader can be assured by the manager that applying a cost/schedule measurement system to her task does not inhibit her freedom to conduct research as she would otherwise.

BASELINE AND REPORTING

After the data gathering has been accomplished, the data must be converted into useable information. At Battelle-Northwest, this is called *preparation of a cost/schedule baseline*. The baseline package may consist of the following: preface, table of contents, work breakdown structure, master schedule, integrated logic network, cost plan, milestone listing, and an explanation of milestones. The cost/schedule baseline is the document against which progress on the program activities will be measured and evaluated.

The research scientist is sometimes very busy and unable to respond readily to requests for data to be included in the baseline package. This may create problems for the program-control specialist who is charged with its preparation. The raw data is collected many times from several research personnel. The specialist, when organizing the data into suitable form, may lack input from only one researcher. The researcher, although not intentionally delaying the data-package preparation, is causing the scheduled completion date to slip. This is often because of his feeling that the technical work is more important and must come first. What action(s) can the program control specialist take to aid in his cause and still not be disruptive in the execution of the technical work?

Of course, the first option would be to put his persuasive talents to work by contacting the researcher and explaining the importance of providing the data on time, when requested. He could cite the program manager's attitude toward the data package scheduled for completion. By using the program manager as a lever, the specialist avoids appearing to be the *bad guy*. He can remind the researcher of his obligation to the program. He can encourage the researcher to lay aside technical work temporarily in order to prepare needed information for the data package. This, the specialist can do and maintain the all-important good working relationships, because he has put himself between the reluctant researcher and the possible displeasure of the program manager.

The second option might be to contact the program manager and suggest a telephone call to the researcher. This option is less desirable because it may carry the inference that the program manager is performing the specialist's job or that the program-control specialist is a spy. As undesirable as this alternative is, it is sometimes necessary. This option may also suggest to the manager a diminished effectiveness of the program-control specialist. This situation should be avoided when possible.

The least-desirable option is to wait for the data to be provided when the researcher has the time. In some instances, however, this may be the only solution. In most cases, the elapsed time involved is not all that long. It may be a day or two, or it may be only an hour or two. In this situation, the program-control specialist may become disturbed by the inhibiting factors that prevent him from performing as desired. If so, he should still maintain a friendly manner, biding his time until the data is available.

After the cost/schedule baseline has been established, the reporting system is addressed. Monthly reports should consist of a technical progress narrative, milestone status, trend curves (which include planned versus actual costs), and planned versus actual percentage of work completed. The actual percentage of work completed will vary subjectively, based on the performer's estimate.

It is difficult to accurately quantify progress in research and development programs. Precise progress measurement is possible on a production line program where, for instance, ten thousand widgets are to be produced. After six thousand widgets have been produced, it could be accurately stated that the program is 60 percent complete.

When quantifying progress, precise accuracy is not normally achievable in research and development programs. However, the program-control specialist should strive for the highest accuracy possible, as accuracy in all reporting is of the utmost importance. Program managers rely on the program-control specialist to provide accurate and timely reports. Nothing can embarrass a manager more than to have her sponsor call her to point out that her report contains erroneous information. Even inconsistent data can be very disturbing. If, when preparing a report, data is detected that might be confusing or inconsistent, this should be addressed in the narrative or in the variance analysis. The monthly report should contain a variance narrative when established thresholds are exceeded. The reporting thresholds are established according to the dollar amount of the program and the work content. At this time, the program-control specialist suggests the program thresholds. Care should be taken to make them not too restrictive. As mentioned previously, when thresholds, sometimes referred to as *tolerance bands*, are too tight, they can cause excessive paperwork in order to explain variances. Many times the variances that require explanations are insignificant, but need clarification solely because unrealistic thresholds are exceeded.

It was previously mentioned that the Air Force uses cost/schedule control-system criteria, which includes *earned value* in its evaluation system. It must be understood that there are varying degrees of subjectivity in assessing progress in the earned-value technique. A lengthy discussion of earned value is not necessary here. It is sufficient to point out that the program-control specialist must understand that a large percentage of progress completion data comes from estimates. The method may not be precisely accurate, but it does provide a percentage measure of progress that can be converted into dollars for comparison with planned and actual cost data. This comparison shows the manager the value of the work performed versus the dollar amount expended. It will tend to reduce subjectivity if properly used.

CHANGE CONTROL SYSTEM

To complete the program-control system, a *system within a system* must be incorporated. This means the establishment of a *change-control system*. The change-control system is designed to provide control and visibility of changes affecting the technical, schedule, and budget baselines. Detailed change-control procedures are normally developed in the management plan. A *change* can be defined as any deviation from approved project documentation including but not limited to technical scope, criteria, drawings, specifications, schedules, budgets, and funds.

The change systems' efforts include:
- recognizing types of changes and sources of change
- evaluating, integrating, and authorizing changes
- maintaining all contract/project logs
- integrating baseline management activity with existing subsystems.

It is well known that changes occur in all programs and projects. Were it not for changes, we would all still be driving Model-T Fords.

A manager of a smaller program may indicate that a formal change-control system is not necessary. He may rely on his own capacity for retention of detail, thereby precluding the necessity for a system. He may also have such a good relationship with the sponsor that he *knows* that he and the sponsor will not encounter problems relating to work scope, schedule, and funding understandings.

The program-control specialist in this circumstance need only mention to the manager that unforeseen events could alter what is currently perceived as a *comfortable situation.* The program-control specialist can illustrate various cases such as personnel transfer, illness, or a catastrophic event such as death by accident or natural causes. Without a change-control system, formal records of agreements will be nonexistent. The effort on the program will possibly be interrupted. It may take time to get the program back on track. With the change-control system providing all of the required detail regarding changes, agreements, and understanding, the program will continue under more favorable conditions.

The change-control system will help avoid snares that can jeopardize the smooth execution of a program or project. The documentation of changes, with appropriate approval signatures, provides a communication link between the sponsor and the performing organization.

The program-control specialist normally assumes, or is assigned to, the *control point* position. As a member of the change-control board, she documents the agreements as to scope, schedule, and funding. The responsibility for preparation of the change documents and obtaining signatures falls into the control point area. The program-control specialist, in her role as control point, maintains the records for the change-control system. The skilled program-control specialist can provide valuable assistance by putting a rough draft of a change document into formal language, thereby relieving the technical personnel of the administrative paperwork. This assumption of responsibility will foster appreciation for her service.

Internal change control is important, as is change control affecting external activities. The basis from which changes are initiated starts with the documents that authorize the work, delineate the scope, set schedules, and designate funding. The authorizing documents are signed by the performer, as well as by the distributor of funds. In this manner, misunderstandings are held to a minimum or eliminated. As requirements for changes emerge, the changes are documented through the change-control system.

It is incumbent upon the program-control specialist to maintain vigilance over the system. She should ensure that all changes are properly described, uniquely identified, logged, and expedited through the signature routine.

In the absence of a change system, alterations in work scope may not include changes in funding. One of the perils appearing to be prevalent is the sponsor defining additional work that the performing organization accepts. When this is done in an informal manner, the requirements are sometimes not precisely defined; additional funding requirements may be slightly referred to or not discussed at all; and the schedule may be ignored completely. The danger is obvious—high risk toward cost overrun and missed scheduled milestones!

The program-control specialist, as a member of the change-control board, must be sure that all parts of a change (scope, schedule, funding) are addressed and thoroughly understood by the agreeing parties.

It is prudent to extend the change-control system to subcontractors, as it allows review and approval of major changes prior to the subcontractor's implementation. In regard to changes that do not require the program manager's approval (small dollar amount), information copies should be forwarded from the subcontractor, thus reserving that all-important line of communication.

An example of what can occur because of the absence of a change-control system is described here; this event actually took place. A subcontractor negotiated a sub-subcontract for a dollar amount 70 percent higher than engineering agreed upon at the time that the prime contract was negotiated with the managing organization. The overcommitment of funds caused the project to overrun to a point when it had to be canceled. Had the change-control system been extended to the subcontractor, information would have flowed to the managing organization, thereby signaling that a review was in order.

The control system for this program had been in effect for only a short time. Had the program control specialist been more aggressive in having the system extended to the subcontractor at the time of its formulation, the *red flag* might have been raised before the overcommitment affected the project. Adjustments might have been made in other areas, which might have allowed the project to continue. Extension of the change-control system to the subcontractor, in this instance, could have prevented project cancellation.

It is important that the change system has the capacity to provide a *trail* of change activity from program initiation to its end. This includes technical, schedule, and budget-change activity.

HUMOR

Does humor have a role in the business of program control? Absolutely! Humor has a role in all aspects of business. Sometimes a *one-liner* can relieve a tense situation, allowing everyone a chuckle before proceeding with the business at hand. Humor should not interfere with the business process and should be used appropriately and sparingly.

SUMMARY

The program-control specialist has a multi-faceted job. There will always be people who will try to find deficiencies in the system— thereby convincing themselves that the system will not work. The program-control specialist has to be a provider of information to personnel who may be averse to change. Some managers have to be shown how a program-control system will benefit them. This task many times falls to the program-control specialist. He should be knowledgeable in all aspects of program control and be a salesman, as well. A system will usually work if people want it to work. Conversely, any system can be *beaten* if someone wants to *beat the system*. But the key person is the program manager, and it is incumbent upon the program-control specialist to gain his confidence so that the manager will encourage his people to allow the system an opportunity to work as it is designed.

Other qualities that can contribute to a program management specialist's success are not directly related to program control. They are rather basic, but very important: communication, manners, and appearance.

These attributes are important to any endeavor; they are brought up here to highlight their importance in the conduct of business. Program control is a business, one that supports technical personnel in achievement of technical goals; hence, it is important to the company's or enterprise's success.

Ideas, when effectively communicated, contribute positively to any effort. In program control, this is essential. Unclear communication can be a barrier to productivity. The program-control specialist must be able to communicate effectively, verbally and in writing. The program-control specialist must also be a *good listener*. She must be able to understand instruction from and anticipate the needs of the manager to whom she provides support. Also, should the need arise, she must precisely understand any communication that will be passed on to others.

Good manners and a good appearance without question garner cooperation. Politeness in delivery, in listening, and when interacting with other personnel can enhance relationships. This will lead to increased cooperation. The following may sound very basic, but *you* like people who treat *you* kindly and politely, and the same is true of people whom *you* treat kindly and politely.

Whether or not the organization employs mandated systems, the roles of the program-control specialist are varied and can include diplomat, tactician, leader, guide, listener, scheduler, budgeter, updater, maintainer, and overall assistant to whomever needs assistance. This support relieves technical people of the burden of administrative paperwork while maintaining control and staying on top of the program.

A successful program-control specialist should have most, if not all, of the qualities described above. Again, these qualities are:

- good technical knowledge of program-control systems and techniques
- even temperament
- sense of humor
- capacity to gain the confidence of supported personnel
- ability to influence people into accepting program control as a way of life
- personality that attracts cooperation from fellow workers
- excelling in communication, both sending and receiving
- maintaining a neat and professional appearance.
- And, finally, as important as any of the above qualities—*good manners.*

References

Department of Defense Instruction 7000.2. 1977 (June 10). Department of Defense Cost/Schedule Control Systems Criteria Joint Implementation Guide. 1976 (Oct. 1): 40, paragraph 2-2.

DOE/CR-0014. 1979 (Aug.). Cost and Schedule Control Systems Criteria for Contract Performance Measurement, Summary Description: 3.

DOE/CR-0015. 1980 (May). Cost and Schedule Control Systems Criteria for Contract Performance Measurement: 1–5.

Patrick, M.G. 1979. Implementing a Project Management System in a Research Laboratory. Presented at the Sixth INTERNET Congress in Bavaria (Sept.) and at the Project Management Institute conference in Atlanta, Georgia, United States (Oct.).

The Rework Cycle: Benchmarks for the Project Manager

Kenneth G. Cooper, Pugh-Roberts Associates/PA Consulting Group, Cambridge, Massachusetts

Project Management Journal 24.1 (March 1993)

Editor's Note: The following article is the third in a three-part series, the first two of which are in the Feb. 1993 issue of *PM Network* where the concept and workings of the rework cycle are introduced. Based on dozens of applications to major development projects, the structure portrays flows of project work in which there are multiple cycles of rework. Rework typically represents the bulk of development project expenditures and time. The absence of its treatment in conventional methods and systems is a critical omission that consistently leads to project overruns. This article translates experience, using the rework cycle *model*, into practical suggestions and guidelines for use by managers of development projects.

WHEN GAUGED BY initial expectations for cost, schedule, and planned product, the prevailing modes of performance on complex development projects are surprise and failure. Conventional methods and systems have contributed to the consistently poor track record of complex project performance. Critical path-based methods lack any consideration of the need for reworking incomplete tasks. Earned-value systems—even those endorsed or required by the government—have been likened, by our contractor clients, to driving a car by watching the rearview mirror. We have

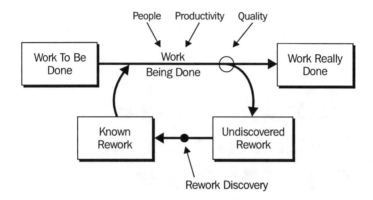

Figure 1   The Structure of the Rework Cycle

developed and applied extensively a structure designed to portray and anticipate the *rework cycle* in development projects.

In Figure 1, the boxes represent pools of work (drawings ... lines of code ... feet of cable). At the start of a project or project stage, all work resides in the pool of *work to be done*. As the project begins and progresses, changing levels of staff (*people*) working at varying *productivity* determine the pace of *work being done*. But unlike all other program/project analysis tools and systems, the rework cycle portrays the real-world phenomenon that work is *executed* at varying but usually less than perfect *quality*. Potentially ranging from 0 to 1, the value of quality (as well as that of productivity) depends on many variable conditions in the project and company. The fractional value of quality determines the portion of the work being done that will enter the pool of *work really done*, which will never again need redoing. The rest will subsequently need some rework, but for a (sometimes substantial) period of time, the rework remains in a pool of what we term *undiscovered rework*— work that contains as-yet-undetected errors and is therefore perceived as being done. Errors are detected by *downstream* efforts or testing; this *rework discovery* may occur months or even years later, during which time dependent work has incorporated these errors or technical derivations thereof. Once discovered, the *known rework* demands the application of resources beyond those needed

Quantifying Quality

This chart shows the empirically derived value of *quality*—the fraction of work being executed that will not require subsequent rework—for dozens of real development projects in different arenas. Along with the range of quality for each industry segment are shown the rework cycles implied by that range. As lower quality causes more cycles of rework, more effort (cost) must be expended to com-

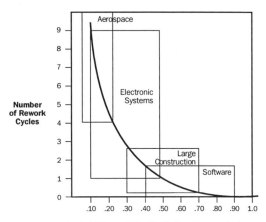

Typical Values of "Quality" in Development Projects

plete the work—the equivalent of doing it once, and then doing it all over again and again. A quality of 0.20 will require five cycles of work and cost (four full rework cycles) to *get it right*.

Development projects here are those that are dominated by design/engineering activity to develop a new product or system, and do not include the building of units to a stable design.

---

for executing the original work. Executed rework enters the flow of work being done, subject to similar productivity and quality variations. Even some of the reworked items may then flow through the rework cycle one or more subsequent times.

For several years, my colleagues and I have been using simulation models[1] based on the rework cycle, and adapting them to accurately recreate, forecast, and diagnose the performance of each of a variety of projects. Across the projects, and within certain groups of projects, have emerged patterns of behavior that can be useful as managerial rules of thumb. While each project is indeed different, the empirical observations and measurements reported here are valid benchmarks for all those who undertake to manage the rework cycle in their own projects.

THE QUALITY RANGE

First, to underscore the magnitude of the issue (and the appropriate degree of managerial concern), consider the range of values exhibited for *quality*—the fraction of work being executed that will not require subsequent rework. As indicated in the sidebar, the effective values range from as high as 0.90 all the way down to below 0.10. The chart in the sidebar shows the range of quality values for each type of project[2] and the resulting number of rework iterations.

Of the projects examined, commercial software development projects exhibited the lowest amount of rework (highest quality), ranging from little rework in some stages to *only* one-and-one-half full rework cycles in others. (Many such projects are actually adaptations of prior developments.) At the other extreme are aerospace development programs—all of these are advanced military developments, usually with substantial research efforts—that typically have at least four (and usually more) rework cycles in the design effort. Between these two extremes are electronic systems development projects (typically designing and integrating systems of new hardware and new software), which exhibit one to nine full rework cycles, and the design of large construction projects, with a range of about one-half to two-and-one-half rework cycles.[3]

Clearly the larger the technological leap being attempted by the overall project, the lower this measure of quality will be (the more rounds of rework). But even within the range of each project type, there is considerable variability in work quality and, therefore, in the cost and time required in a development project. Consider the project performance improvement achievable with even moderate improvements in quality! In an era when 30–40 percent performance improvements are set forth as ambitious targets for organizations undergoing *change programs* and *process reengineering*, the highly leveraged impact of this kind of *quality improvement* must not be overlooked.

THE REWORK DISCOVERY TIME

Still, no matter what the quality improvement effort and impact, undetected errors and rework cycles are unavoidable in complex development projects. With whatever rework is generated, it has its most destructive effect on the whole project when it is in the state of *undiscovered rework*. Discovering the rework earlier and faster removes much of the programwide disruption, especially the development time impacts.

To illustrate this, we used our model of the rework cycle to simulate the development time required for a project under varying levels of quality *and* the speed of rework discovery. Figure 2 summarizes the results in terms of the multiple of the original work schedule. (For convenience, think of a development effort planned to achieve initial work completion in one year—the results shown in Figure 2 would then be *number of years*.)

The chart shows four lines—for rework discovery times equal to one-quarter of the original design plan time (one-fourth year in our example), as well as discovery times of one-half, three-quarters, and one.

As is now obvious, improvement either in quality or rework discovery yields much better schedule performance. It is noteworthy from the results charted that lowering the rework discovery time in an organization or project is most leveraged in improving schedule performance when quality is not at extremely low or extremely high levels. At extremely high quality levels, there simply isn't as much room for improvement of schedule performance. And, in the stages of a development when extremely low quality prevails, rapid rework discovery ends up subjecting the execution of the discovered rework to the same low quality conditions that caused it to cycle in the first place! *In such conditions, it is best to work first on quality-enhancement practices and systems, then to accelerate the benefit with rework discovery enhancements*—such as earlier or improved reviews or testing.

MEASURING WHERE YOU STAND

The prevailing rework discovery time on design development efforts is typically in the range of one-fourth to three-fourths the scheduled length of the original design effort. In order to derive a good approximation of rework discovery times, construct a graph of the issues and reissues of the work product in the stage of development being examined (historically, if available; otherwise, monitor an ongoing effort). Graph over time each subsequent round of

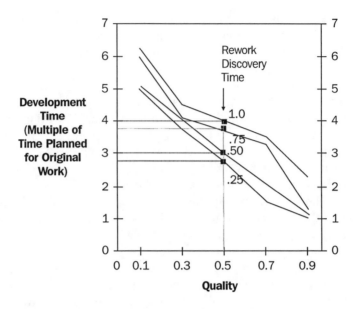

Figure 2 For most levels of work quality, improving the rework discovery time yields significant improvements in development schedules.

revision as a line. Simplified, your chart should look comparable to that in Figure 3.

By measuring the typical horizontal *distance* (time) between each adjacent pair of curves, good estimates of the rework discovery time (and how it changes over the project/stage) may be obtained.

Now you can also compute a good approximation of the time-varying quality of a project stage's work product. Calculate the ratio of the number of revisions to the number of releases/revisions in the prior round, then subtract each computed ratio from 1.0. For example, if there were 350 "Revision B's" on 500 "Revision A's," the prevailing quality during the work on Revision As was: $1 - (350/500) = 1 - 0.70 = 0.30$.[4]

Are You Lost in the Triangle?

Armed with this new information, you will be able to assess where your project stands relative to other development projects. Further,

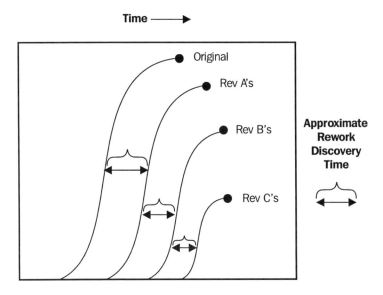

Figure 3   A critical addition to the set of closely monitored project performance measures should be the magnitude and timing of work revisions.

you will be able to determine much more accurately where your project really stands *as it proceeds.*

We used our simulation model of the rework cycle to construct the charts in Figures 4 and 5, which are necessary for more correct mid-project assessments of progress and the magnitude of remaining effort. Using your estimates of project quality and rework discovery time to select the appropriate chart, one may *look up* the true (range of) real progress. In fact, with the benefit of data on a completed project, one may construct one's own *progress ramp* chart by plotting for the completed project: the historically reported *percent complete* versus a retrospective computation of the percent *really* complete then. (You should compute the percent really complete based on hours spent to that point, relative to the total hours eventually spent.)

Perfectly accurate project progress monitoring would yield a straight 45° diagonal (hence the triangular ramp shape): at a perceived/reported condition of 20 percent complete, the actual percent complete would be 20 percent, and so on. Instead, real progress is typically less than reported progress. Further, a given level of reported

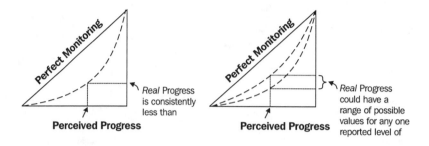

Figure 4   Progress ramps help identify the true state of progress on a project or project phase.

progress might mean any of a range of values for real progress, as shown in Figure 4.

Shown in Figure 5 for each of three typical combinations of quality and rework discovery time are the relations between perceived percent complete as reported by traditional systems, and the real percent complete when undiscovered rework is taken into account. In every case, there is a gap between real progress and perceived progress. Looking across the three charts, it becomes clear that the *lower the quality and the longer the rework discovery times*:

■   the larger the gap between real progress and that which is perceived, and the longer lasting the gap

■   the later in the project/stage that a significant gap persists

■   the greater and longer lasting the *uncertainty* in the size of the gap

■   the later the point of maximum uncertainty about real progress.

THE 90 PERCENT SYNDROME

The demonstrated uncertainty in real progress is responsible for several well-known troublesome project phenomena. One is the *90 percent syndrome* in which, for a prolonged time, project managers report to executives or to the customer that efforts are 90 percent done. Examine the middle-progress ramp in Figure 5 for an example of this. In these conditions, an earnest, responsible manager might well report 90 percent progress achieved, when 75 or 80 percent is really done. And so it goes until, after much distress and disappointment (and time and cost), 90 percent is really achieved,

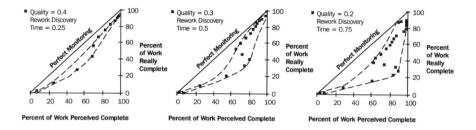

Figure 5   Lower quality and longer rework discovery times disguise low real progress, and increase the range of uncertainty in progress estimation.

and the project moves on to completion. Quite apart from any lily-gilding inclinations of engineers, there is a systemic cause for the 90 percent syndrome.

THE LOST YEAR

One of our clients managing a large new system development project described (not calmly) a related phenomenon and requested a diagnosis. The 1,000-person development effort had progressed to what seemed about two-thirds to three-quarters completion. *One year later,* after an additional one thousand staff-years of effort, it seemed that they had made no progress, or had even lost ground, followed by a slow pace of progress toward completion. He called it the "lost year." His question: "What happened?" The abbreviated answer is clear once again from the middle-progress ramp. In these conditions, 70 percent progress could be reported as *early,* as at 30 percent real progress. Quite some time later (specifically, one year), having made 25–30 percent more real progress, *the system* can still be reporting 70 percent progress, or even less.

What happened? A lot of progress was made. A lot of rework was found and corrected (work that had been viewed as *done*). The lost year wasn't lost; it obviously felt like *one step forward, one step back,* but it was just a large example of the rework cycle thwarting conventional monitoring systems. Even after the lost year, the project, still being reported at about 70 percent complete, was in fact just 60

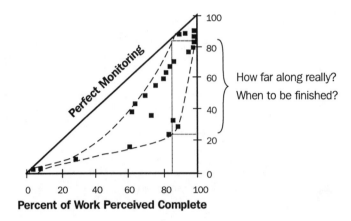

Figure 6   The end can appear to be near when real progress is as low as 30 percent, leading to overly optimistic product introduction plans, destined to be delayed.

percent complete, so what was seen as the remaining 30 percent felt like it took a long time to finish.

THE DELAYED PRODUCT INTRODUCTION

Not so very uncommon was the dilemma faced by another client firm. It wanted to introduce its new system product at the earliest responsible time in a technologically competitive market. But it had a history of undependable announcements on product release schedules, followed by dashed expectations. When could it really promise the market that this new system product would be available?

The diagnosis revealed a somewhat higher quality than in the prior charts, but with a longer rework discovery time, as characterized by the third progress ramp (shown again in Figure 6). In this condition, the true status of a development project remains highly uncertain until the very end. Combined with consistent overestimation of progress are wide (vertical) bands of uncertainty within which perceived progress may become unexpectedly *stuck*. While real progress is being made, the late and prolonged appearance of previously undiscovered rework results in ever-sliding, undependable estimates of completion time—particularly at the later stages, when companies are making announcements of new product introduction schedules.

This client's organization and practices had been set so as to encourage high levels of *completion* before subjecting to testing the integrated prototype. The analysis led the client to implement a new structure and set of procedures, which included much more testing earlier. While this increased testing costs, total project time and costs were reduced significantly. And, although the resulting earlier rework discovery was a bit *scary* to the managers at first, much more dependable introduction schedules were attained.

CONCLUSION

Despite the need for advances in the stagnated theory and practice of development project management, no new gimmicks, no new software, will significantly improve development projects' performance. Rather, we need to improve our fundamental understanding of how projects really work. A healthy start is understanding the critical role of the rework cycle. It must be recognized, monitored, and minimized—and if it is, we can eventually achieve dramatic breakthroughs in project costs and schedules.

Documented herein is the range of quality and rework in different projects, how to monitor quality and the rework discovery time, and how to translate these newly collected measures into more accurate project progress assessments. They are necessary but only the most basic steps toward a more strategic and realistic view of projects.

Even with *a better model*, there will remain a managerial inertia forged from years, even decades, of misunderstanding. It will not be enough for project managers to internalize the associated lessons of the rework cycle. They must also learn the important differences between the substantial *influence* that the manager has over productivity, quality, and rework discovery (and hence, project costs and schedules), and the relative lack of *control* that the manager has over these same conditions. Understanding how the actions that managers can take influence their projects' outcomes requires extensions beyond the basic rework cycle structure. The very best of project managers know these intuitively. But, just as important, managers' formulated action plans and their logic must be effectively and persuasively communicated to (and implemented with the aid of) many other players—senior company managers and colleagues, the project staff, partners and suppliers, and customers themselves. The passive manager (or worse, those who encourage obfuscating or ostrich-like behavior) will not make waves—nor will they make any contribution. Their projects will continue to fail. Successful project managers will take on the roles of thought leader and action leader—the advocate and instrument of change in the systems and practices that surround them. The alternative—the unmitigated machination of the rework cycle—will mean continuing the familiar pattern of development projects: unforeseen costs, unexpected delays, and unfulfilled promises.

Notes

1. These project models were built using the dynamic continuous simulation language DYNAMO; see *DYNAMO User's Manual*, Pugh-Roberts Associates, and *Introduction to Systems Dynamics Modeling with DYNAMO*, George P. Richardson and Alexander L. Pugh III.
2. We acknowledge the bias in the data caused by the fact that easy, smoothly running projects rarely command the attention of consultants brought in by management. Therefore, the true range of quality values is likely to be broader *to the right* for each class if one includes less difficult projects.
3. Take heart, homebuilders: the construction projects in the sample reported here—power plants, combatant ships—all significantly exceed $1 billion.
4. Technical content and organizational practice in executing and reporting revisions vary widely. Account should be taken of the fact that the amount of effort on successive rounds of revisions will change (usually decrease). All measures of quality reported herein have been normalized to represent revision effort that is equal to original releases on a per unit basis.

The $2,000 Hour: How Managers Influence Project Performance Through the Rework Cycle

Kenneth G. Cooper, Pugh-Roberts Associates/PA Consulting Group, Cambridge, Massachusetts

Project Management Journal 25.1 (March 1994)

IF THOSE OF us who manage projects have proven one thing, it is that we know how to fail. After all, we do it consistently. A worldwide survey conducted in 1992 showed clearly what we all suspected: The majority of all development projects fail to meet their time and cost targets.[1]

For those whose business is projects—construction firms, defense contractors, design agents—the business impacts are obvious, large, and bad. For all other technology-intensive companies, the effects on business—revenue, growth, profits, market share, reputation—are just as large and just as bad.

Computer hardware and software companies miss projected new product introduction dates with such regularity that on-time performance is news. Automobile companies struggle to reduce new car development costs and time, so as to compete more effectively. Banks, insurance firms, and other service institutions conduct in-house or contracted development efforts to improve their operational efficiency and quality. Telecommunications companies compete in an increasingly complex arena through system development efforts that aim to reduce costs, expand services, and broaden product offerings.

Is all of the attention and effort worth it? One of our consulting clients, a major contractor, estimated that the firm's profits and stockholder value would *double* if development project overruns were more effectively contained. *Business Week* cites Thomas P. Hustad, editor of the *Journal of Product Innovation Management*, observing that "companies that lead their industries in profitability and sales growth get 49 percent of their revenues from products developed in the past five years. The least successful get only 11 percent of sales from new products."[2] Is all the attention and effort working? As noted in the MIT-PA survey, not particularly well. Development project management continues to fail regularly, sometimes spectacularly, *because managers consistently fail to see how their actions affect project performance.*

BRIEF ADVICE TO CUSTOMERS, EXECUTIVES, AND PROJECT MANAGERS

This article is targeted at all the project customers who have sat by, chagrined over ever-growing cost estimates and ever-slipping completion date targets, or who have jumped in themselves to *help* manage. It is for the company executives who have listened to project managers report—first glowingly, then sadly—the state of key development efforts, and who set the business policies and environment within which those projects must be executed. And this article is for every project manager who must deal with the aforementioned while working with independent-minded engineers, otherwise-incentivized matrix department heads, remote vendors, and even consultants and lawyers in a dozen meetings a day, all to try and manage a project that is underfunded, tightly scheduled, understaffed, and closely watched, to develop a product that is technically ambitious, ill-defined, and probably critical to the success of the company.

To those customers, executives, and managers: *Stop what you're doing now.* There is an excellent chance that what you learned from simpler projects, textbooks, courses, and "accepted practice"—or what you are feeling pressured to do in response to problems—is *wrong.*

Worse than ineffective, many traditional managerial responses and rules of thumb actually *aggravate* project performance problems. We will examine herein several examples of how managers *intend* to affect projects, and the nearly universal *secondary* side effects that routinely thwart this intent. We will see:

- How managers regularly and unknowingly spend $2,000 and more for each additional person-hour of effective work.
- When *extending* a schedule can save money ... and *time*.
- Why getting staffed up to a fast start can hurt your project performance.
- Another butchered sacred cow or two.

But My Project Is Different

Having worked to help some seventy large projects and programs, I have heard that statement begun approximately seventy times. It is an awfully convenient notion to be able to lay blame for an overrun on some *thing*. It is seductively comforting to cite as this project's uniquely difficult problem:

- that troublesome part of the generator/radar/chip/hydraulics/ test program/subroutine/etc.
- the awful problems obtaining enough qualified labor for the (*fill in your favorite technical trouble spot here*
- the vendor of that key component going out of business/being late/not meeting specs
- all those last-minute design/spec changes the customer/top brass/engineers insisted upon.

In managing projects, we can externalize with the best of them, laying responsibility for poor performance on some tangible external source peculiar to that project. But one—often more than one—of the above conditions occurs on *every* complex project. And, indeed, all of them do contribute, sometimes mightily, to cost and schedule problems. But so long as we attribute blame exclusively to individual project circumstances as though they were unique, we prevent ourselves from learning true systemic *causes* and transferable project management lessons.

This mindset is partly attributable to the suite of conventional project management tools and systems in place. Critical Path Method (CPM)-based tools describe a project as a networked sequence of discrete technical tasks and events. Earned value-based "cost and schedule control"[3] systems portray a project as the sum of discrete work segments. Such tools and systems can be badly misleading by failing to portray that projects really do not work in a straight line of tasks started and ended, but in an iterative process of accomplishment. Further, they encourage the view of projects as projectiles, hurtling toward an outcome (eventually) on which human intervention has little effect.

As managers, we need to (and the best do) run our projects with two viewpoints that are very different from conventional ones, as follows.

1. Every stage, and most tasks, of our projects will have cycles of rework, even if the precise content is yet to be discovered.

2. Although we have little absolute control, we have enormous *influence* on project performance. Our decisions and actions work through multiple *cause-effect paths* to affect the rework cycle (see sidebar) and the project outcome.

THE $2,000 HOUR

We all know managers who have agonized over one or two percentage-point differences in salary or wage changes for individuals, amounting to less than a dollar an hour. The same managers will, without a second thought (indeed, without knowing) pay $2,000 or more for each effective hour of work when that work is performed by project staff working extended *overtime*.

Figure 1 adds to the rework cycle structure a *path* showing a chain of cause-effect relationships, indicated by the solid arrows. Using information from the *pools* of work in the rework cycle (but without knowing, of course, the size or content of as-yet-undiscovered rework), managers or their aides periodically estimate the progress made to date in the project, or in a stage of the project. Based on this, they assess the extent to which additional staffing is needed to try to finish the remaining work on the prevailing schedule. A common and reasonable response to an indication that one is falling behind schedule is to supplement the effective staffing, in terms of full-time equivalent (FTE) people, by the temporary use of overtime. This avoids the cost, hassle, and long-term commitment of bringing in additional people through hiring or transfer.

The Rework Cycle

Introduced in the February 1993 issue of *PM Network*, the rework cycle structure portrays flows of project work, be it for feet of cable, tons of steel, lines of code, design drawings, and so on. The structure is the core of a simulation model developed for and applied to dozens of complex design and construction projects (power plants,

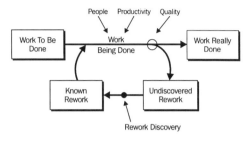

aerospace developments, electronics, software systems, shipbuilding, and so on).

At the start of a project or project stage, all work resides in the pool of *work to be done*. As the project begins and progresses, changing levels of *people* working at varying *productivity* levels determines the pace of *work being done*. But, unlike all other program/project analysis tools and systems, the rework cycle portrays the real-world phenomenon that work is executed at varying but usually less than perfect levels of *quality*. A fraction that potentially ranges from 0 to 1.0, the value of quality (as well as that of productivity) depends on many variable conditions in the project and company. The fractional value of quality determines the portion of the work being done that will enter the pool of *work really done*, which will never again need redoing. The *rest* will subsequently need some rework, but, for a (sometimes substantial) period of time, the rework remains in a pool of what we term *undiscovered rework*—work that contains as-yet-undetected errors and is therefore *perceived* as being done. Errors are detected by *downstream* efforts or testing; this *rework discovery* may occur months or even years later, during which time dependent work has incorporated these errors or technical derivations thereof. Once discovered, the *known rework* demands the application of people beyond those needed for completing the original work. Executed rework enters the flow of work being done, subject to similar productivity and quality variations. Even some of the reworked items may then flow through the rework cycle one or more subsequent times.

The full simulation models of these development projects employ thousands of equations. They explicitly portray the time-varying conditions that cause changes in productivity, quality, staffing levels, rework detection, and work execution, as well as the interdependencies among multiple project stages. All of the dynamic conditions at work in these projects and their models—e.g., staff experience levels, work sequence, supervisory adequacy, *spec* stability, worker morale, task feasibility, vendor timeliness, overtime, schedule pressure, hiring and attrition, progress monitoring, organization and process changes, prototyping, testing, and so forth—cause changes, some more directly than others, in the performance of the rework cycle. Because our business clients require demonstrable accuracy in the models upon which they will base important decisions, we need to develop accurate measures of all these factors, especially those of the rework cycle itself.

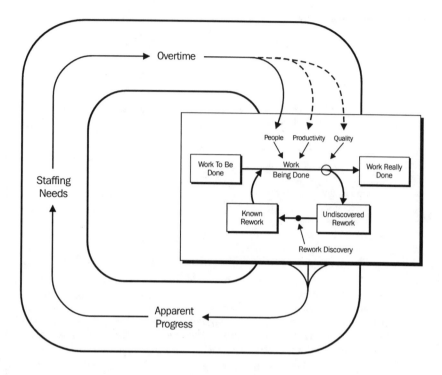

Figure 1 Paths of Influence from the Use of Overtime

But a few weeks of overtime easily extends into more sustained overtime usage, as a key milestone approaches, or as the schedule gap stubbornly refuses to close (e.g., with the continuing discovery of more rework to do). As a purposeful choice, or because the *end* remains tantalizingly (and misleadingly) close, the overtime is continued. The intended direct effect (increasing the FTE people) is achieved. However, the *secondary* effect (through fatigue) on worker productivity and work quality, though often acknowledged in spirit, is consistently underestimated. (This path of unintended secondary influence is shown in the diagram with dashed arrows.)

The set of plots in Figure 2 displays results from two different executions of the same project. (The results shown are for a typical design stage in this example, but similar results occur in production/construction.) It is a four-year project with a labor budget of some $50 million, planned for 500,000 hours of design effort over three years, and 800,000 hours of construction (or initial production).

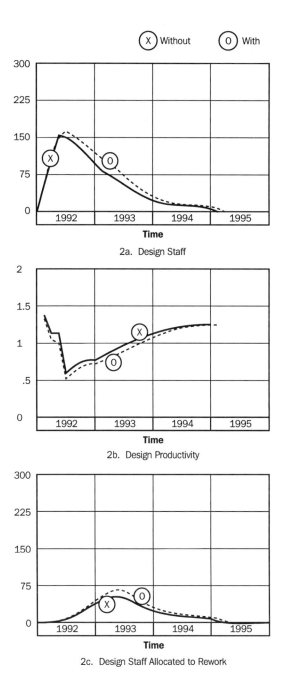

2a. Design Staff

2b. Design Productivity

2c. Design Staff Allocated to Rework

Figure 2 The Project, With the Secondary Effects of Overtime

We used our project simulation model (see sidebar) to generate the performance of the project under two different conditions. Results from the first simulation (labeled X in each of the charts) display what occurs in the design effort with typical overtime usage, but only with the intended direct effect on FTE staffing—no unintended secondary effects on productivity or work quality. In other words, this is an artificial—and unrealistic—world (but one that often seems to be the view of some managers). In the second simulation, labeled O in each of the charts), we activate the secondary influences of overtime, at the strength of effect that we have observed operating in dozens of development projects.

In 2a of Figure 2, the plots of design staffing, clearly shows that additional effort is required to finish the same design tasks when the secondary effects are at work. In fact, the cumulative effort is 15–20 percent greater, or some 60,000 hours—that's more than thirty person-*years* of effort—in this example.

The causes of the extra effort required are clear from the plotted results in 2b and 2c in Figure 2. In 2b, the per-person productivity[4] drops as a result of overtime-induced fatigue. And the parallel effect of lowered work *quality* is the cause of more rework effort (about 25 percent more), as shown in 2c. The actual amount of overtime used in the two simulations is about the same, but its real effects drive up program costs significantly

All right, you say, we know it's expensive, but we're trying to meet a schedule here! Well, it might be worth the extra $3 million cost of the design effort, if only it helped the schedule. Instead, the work requires an *additional* two months of time to reach completion, largely as a result of the added rework cycling.

Recently, a defense contractor client's CFO wanted to establish an explicit, cost-effective policy on overtime for the company. We were asked to use our simulation model and the numerical factors established for several complex system design-and-build projects to determine guidelines for overtime usage. We calculated the cost of each effective full hour of output, when productivity and rework *penalties* were taken into account. Figure 3 summarizes the results for engineering and production staff working sustained overtime (for two to three months or more) at a level of four, eight, and twelve hours per week (per person).

At a sustained level of four hours per week, both engineering and production staff achieve one-and-a-half to two hours worth of real, effective extra work output. At a sustained eight hours per

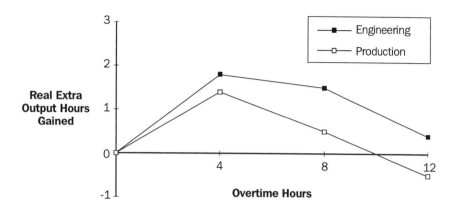

Figure 3   Real Output from Different Levels of Sustained Overtime

week, the fatigue effect sets in more strongly for build workers than engineers, understandably. Even those engaged in engineering efforts, however, achieve less output than when working just four hours sustained overtime; those in production achieve only a half-hour of effective extra output beyond a standard forty-hour week! At twelve hours per week sustained overtime, engineers nearly match that low extra output performance, while those in production actually output less than in a standard no-overtime week.

If managers are paying wages for the overtime hours, perhaps even an overtime premium, the cost for each effective hour of output achieved is staggering. In the most benign condition, achieving about two extra output hours for four overtime hours, each extra output hour costs about $150 (4 hours x $50/hour x 1.5 overtime premium = $300; $300/2 output hours = $150/output hour). At twelve hours per week sustained overtime, engineers' extra 0.4 hour of output (1 percent beyond a forty-hour week) costs a total of 45 percent more than the cost of a forty-hour week—an effective cost of over *$2,000 per hour of gained output*.[5]

The pattern is similar but even more extreme for production, yielding a cost of *infinity* per extra hour of real output with twelve hours per week of sustained overtime—less real extra output at a greater cost than a standard work week. In the production efforts analyzed, the *cross-over point* to no net extra work from sustained overtime appears at about the ten-hour mark;[6] for engineers, the cross-over point is (just) beyond twelve hours. But for both groups

67

of workers, even four weekly hours of sustained overtime is *more* expensive than conventionally figured, and more sustained overtime yields *less* total output.

IT'S THE LAW

With sustained overtime being such a costly and unattractive option, the need for additional resources usually turns managers to hiring (or transferring) additional people onto a project. Hardly unavoidable at the start or in moderation, bringing new people into a project organization has a degree of secondary impact that is, again, widely underestimated or ignored. But the impacts—potentially harsh ones—will occur nonetheless

In the classic book *The Mythical Man-Month*,[7] the author offers Brooks's Law: "Adding manpower to a late software project makes it later." Admittedly a simplification with exceptions, it still captures the spirit of a very real and damaging set of phenomena.

The diagram in Figure 4 shows another set of cause-effect paths of influence that work over the course of time, when managers decide to hire in response to a perceived need for additional staff. The obvious intent is to bring in new people who will supplement the existing staff, increasing the FTE headcount available to work the project.

With any substantial hiring or even transferring of people unfamiliar with the project, the new people enter with less experience or skill than those already on board .(Despite individual exceptions, this holds true, especially for technically demanding work or specialized skill needs.) So the average skill level of the growing staff drops, at least long enough for new people to *get up to speed*, which can take years. Worse, the more hiring occurs in any constrained labor market, the lower the entry-skill level will be (assuming you're hiring the most appropriately talented first). It's as though you are hiring from a *barrel* of eligible candidates, and the more you take, the closer you come to scraping the bottom of the barrel. And the longer it will take to bring along the latest entries.

As if that were not enough, there is an added *kicker*. Newly hired individuals tend to have a higher attrition rate than longer-time, experienced people—from mistakes in hiring, recruitment expectations not met, less loyalty, wanderlust, and so on. A higher attrition

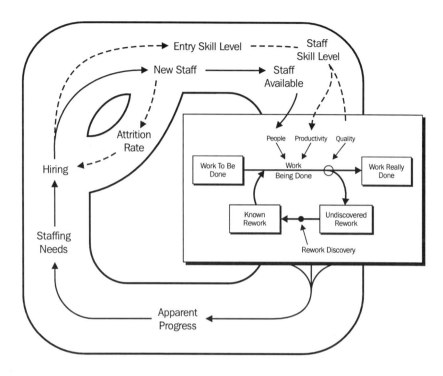

Figure 4   Paths of Influence from New Employee Hiring

rate requires still more new hiring, just to remain even—let alone expand the staff more. So a vicious circle develops, a *churning* with little forward progress, while new people are hired, departure rates increase, and still more new people are hired to sustain the organization.

It gets worse still. Any problem response that in turn adversely affects productivity or quality, such as lowered skill levels from hiring (or sustained overtime fatigue, for that matter) can trigger a sinister set of self-reinforcing impacts on a circular path of cause and effect. As the same diagram indicates, the hiring, which yields skill-worsened productivity and quality, slows the pace of progress relative to the schedule (especially as the additional rework generated by less skilled people is discovered). With less than planned progress, we clearly need … more people! Thus, more hires, new people, skill dilution, productivity and quality reduction, slowed progress, and so on. Lest you think this is an academic concoction, be assured that we have observed this exact phenomenon in many organizations—it starts innocently and builds insidiously, becoming a trap into which one can easily fall.

In engineering control terms, it's called a positive feedback loop (*positive* because it's self-reinforcing), but there's nothing positive about its effect on the project cost. Even the schedule-remedying intent can be thwarted by the addition of a cycle or two of extra rework required as a result of the reduced work quality. Hence, Brooks's Law, to which we can add the equally simplified and immodestly named Cooper's Corollary: *adding (many) people to a late development project makes it cost more—lots more.*

We haven't even mentioned the added strain on supervisors, extra coaching and training time invested by experienced staff, and the disruption of a rapidly growing organization. We'll turn on these effects, along with the skill level path of influence, in the next simulations of the same project, the results of which are plotted in Figure 5.

Building on the conditions of the previous simulation (which contained the effects of overtime usage), we make this an even more realistic simulation of the project by adding the secondary effects of hiring new people. Again, it's the same project otherwise; we're just comparing the performance on the project in the (unreal) world of no skill consequences (labeled O) to the (more real) world that includes them (labeled S).

Unsurprisingly now, the adverse secondary effects cause a much higher expenditure of labor (see 5a in Figure 5). Not only is productivity lower throughout (5b), but we also devote even more effort to rework (5c). In fact, total hours climb by 190,000 (up 45 percent), and more rework accounts for nearly two-thirds of that increase. Indeed, the rework effort here is nearly half of the total hours spent on the design.

Not only is there more effort, but the added rework cycling extends the time of performance by another three months in design (and—though not shown here—in the build effort, as well). In a particularly vicious circle, the additional delay induces the managers to employ more overtime, too—now over 50,000 hours' worth—thus incurring even more secondary impacts on productivity and work quality (and cost and schedule).[8]

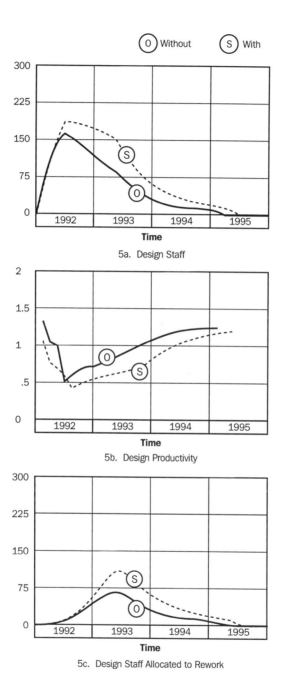

5a. Design Staff

5b. Design Productivity

5c. Design Staff Allocated to Rework

Figure 5   The Project, With the Secondary Effects of Hiring

Do You Have a Reservation?

True progress in development efforts is inherently difficult to assess, so, understandably, we have devised surrogate measures that are easier to monitor during the conduct of projects. We count drawings issued, lines or segments of code written, the earned value of milestones met, or even simply hours spent, as approximations of true work progress made. The problem is that having been taught, or feeling obligated (and under pressure), to be precise, we consistently make the mistake of believing such estimates—and taking action based on them. While they certainly are *precise* (793 drawings, 45.2 percent, and so forth), they are not *accurate*. It's like measuring time with a much-too-fast digital watch—quite a precise display of 4:52, but three significant digits are superfluous when you cannot even trust the first to be accurate.[9]

In deciding how and when to staff, we too often depend on the precise but inaccurate *digital watch* when we assess the readiness of prerequisite work products to support the execution of the next dependent tasks. The *bean count* of prerequisite work done may indicate we can staff up on the dependent stage of work. But we need to take better account—even if approximate—of the quality of the work logged as *done* when making staffing decisions. The quality of that work—specifically here the extent to which it will or will not need reworking—is important to gauge, because staffing and working dependent tasks will incorporate the same errors, or derivations thereof, and thus create more rework cycling in the downstream efforts as well.

The prerequisite work may take any of several forms—design information on drawings, customer-supplied information or equipment, vendor products, software specs, steel framing, electronic circuitry, and so on. In the case of engineering drawings, some contractors annotate known missing segments or information with a "reservation."[10] Despite the reservation, however, the drawing is counted as released, and the dependent efforts (within the design stages, or in procurement, or in production) are staffed as though the tally of drawings reflects work really done.

The diagram in Figure 6 displays this additional pathway through which management decisions affect projects and their rework cycle. In determining appropriate staffing levels, managers consider the apparent availability of prerequisite tasks' work products. But poor

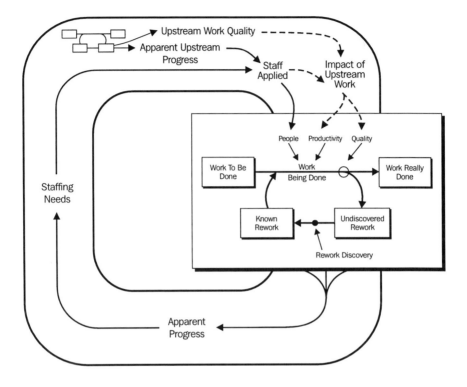

Figure 6   Paths of Influence from Staffing on Low-Quality Work

quality of that prerequisite work will cause unintended reductions in subsequent productivity and work quality. And the more aggressively the project (or stage) is staffed in this condition, the more people and work that are subject to these adverse impacts.

Now let's add to the simulation of the *same project* these unintended but real productivity and quality effects caused by staffing dependent work while *quality* problems remain in upstream work products. The performance results are shown in Figure 7, contrasted with the prior simulation.

The new simulation (labeled Q on the plots) is an even more realistic model of the project than the prior simulation (labeled S), in which just the overtime and skill dilution effects were present. And, as the realism builds, so too do the project costs (now up an additional 40 percent) and time (four months later still).

The plot of staffing (see 7a in Figure 7) reflects both consequences, and now exhibits an all-too-familiar shape. What had been, at the start of the whole sequence, a fairly *normal* (idealized, really) staffing profile now displays a second *hump* (in mid-1993) more than six months later than the first. This is characteristic of many a troubled project (or stage).

Having staffed up (too) rapidly when prerequisite work products were of low quality (i.e., high rework content), the *knock on* effect on the quality[11] of this stage of work is significant (see the comparative plots of work quality in 7b). This causes another large increase in rework effort (7c), which peaks in mid-1993, and causes the staffing to *double hump*. Indeed, not only is rework up (another 170,000 hours), it is up disproportionately (it is nearly three-quarters of the total increase in—the rest from reduced productivity). Rework now accounts for over 50 percent of the design effort. In other words, the simulation has become sufficiently realistic as to behave like most difficult development projects.

The especially aggravating characteristic of these effects is that they are really quite insidious. There are no routinely monitored factors, no accurate *index of leading problematic indicators*, no handy standard warning bells, to tell us we're going wrong. Without improvements in our ability to detect and estimate rework (and reduce it), our normal progress monitoring measures just do not tell us soon enough how we're doing.

It's the chip. We have *cut off* the post-1992 segments of this most recent simulation in Figure 8, charting design staff (8a) and the apparent progress (8b—the fraction of work perceived to be complete takes no account of yet-to-be-discovered rework). This is what you would be seeing one year into the project. Sure, the current staffing is higher than the plan, but we've spent about 300,000 hours to achieve what we perceive (hope) to be about 60 percent completion. A little arithmetic says we should finish design near the 500,000-hour budget, and that means we should be able to staff down soon, and quickly.

How many times have you sat in a progress briefing and listened to or seen the *current operating plan* depict the future staffing returning to the *on-budget* line? Why, sometimes it almost seems preordained that way. Contrast those plans with the reality, as shown in 8c and 8d.

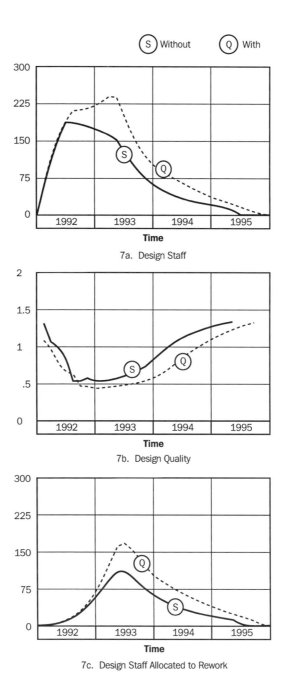

Figure 7   The Project, With the Secondary Effects of Low-Quality Work

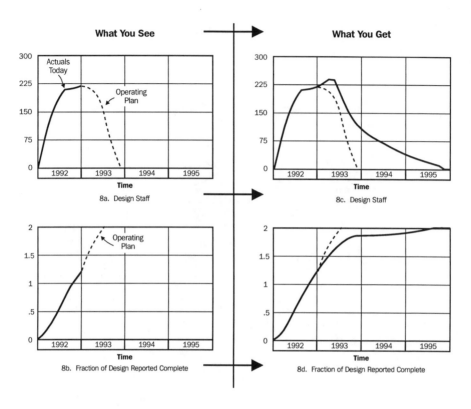

Figure 8 Dashed Hopes

Where are the problems that cause the apparent progress to stall near 90 percent for over a year, while design expenditures eventually rise to well over the 800,000-hour mark? Why, it must be the unique-to-this-project problem we have with that troublesome part of the generator/radar/chip/hydraulics/subroutine/vendor. (That is, as opposed to any systemic flaw in our ability to monitor and manage rework, from which we would be able to draw transferable lessons to achieve true organizational learning and long-term project and business performance improvement—nah, it's the chip).

Customers and company executives take heed. Those of us to whom project managers report, whether inside the organization or as paying customers, are very often the most guilty parties. Eager to see progress on an important development, we commit one of two serious errors, as described below.

1. We micro-manage, instructing the project manager to staff up (prematurely)—not knowing any better ourselves. Or we *effectively* do so by criticizing the manager (or as a customer, the manager's executive) for failing to staff up (enough/according to plan/in the face of missing a near-term schedule milestone). We assert that the low staffing will "jeopardize the future of the project," and we lay the basis for, or induce the fear of, retribution. Retribution can take many forms—job loss or demotion, delayed payments, disallowed costs, the prospect of losing future business, intransigence on a variety of to-be-approved or -negotiated items, even legal claims. All this when the smartest, best thing to do for the project cost and *final* completion schedule is to restrain staffing temporarily.[12]

2. We create an environment or relationship through intimidation in which the project manager, if he wishes to remain employed, knows better than to *own up* to prior work not *really* being ready. Thus, the project manager staffs as though the prior work had no problems.

My colleagues and I have analyzed dozens of difficult projects, and a case where one or both of these conditions is *not* present is the exception—the rare exception.

YOUR PARENTS WERE RIGHT ALL ALONG

True story: A group of bright young managers were in a company training course being prepared for the rigors of taking on full program management responsibilities. Confronted with a scenario in which the program they were *managing* was falling behind schedule, they were asked about their responses to this prospect. The glee in their eyes was visible, their excitement palpable. Throughout the responses was the nearly unanimous feeling, expressed by one young buck, who had observed and absorbed the way things really work, "We really turn the screws on the engineers."

Not everything we do as managers involves a tangible action. What we say and the *incidental* gestures we make influence the people around us, and the people who work for them, more than we know—or is it exactly as we know? To exert schedule pressure on those around us is a natural, and nearly universal, managerial response to lagging progress. A little bit is good, sharpening the senses and increasing productivity. But like unsolicited criticism, a little goes a long way.

The diagram in Figure 9 demonstrates the intended path of influence of schedule pressure—an increase in productivity. It also shows the unwanted side effects. At some point in your childhood, someone, probably your mother or father, told you that *haste makes waste*—usually after you just finished rushing through something only to find you made a mistake. You now have to rework it with more effort than would have been required if you had taken the care to do it right the first time.

Despite the slogan posters prevalent on the walls of project offices—"If you don't have time to do it right the first time, where will you find the time to do it again?"—it does not seem we've learned the lesson our parents tried to so hard to deliver. *The harder I work, the behinder I get* is the worker's response to the slogan posters. But, work hard (and fast) they do, knowing managers want to see *product*. The quality impact (the later need to do it again) is far less visible, but no less real.

Equally real are longer-term impacts of sustained pressures. Every experienced manager has seen the considerable morale impacts when the staff is pressured from all sides to improve not only on the schedule, but also on the costs and the quality. Before he retired, Walt Maguire was one of the great program managers and had led several big aerospace programs at Hughes Aircraft Company. He said he tried to think of those three dimensions as an elastic triangle—you could push and squeeze on any two sides, but the other side would then have to "give." Push on schedule and quality, and cost gives, and so on. But you cannot (should not) squeeze all three sides at once—the impracticality of it just generates friction, frustration, and, eventually, a demoralizing effect that saps people's productivity—even work quality.

Beyond these secondary effects on productivity and quality, Figure 9 depicts yet another cause-effect pathway of influence often activated by schedule pressure. In such a highly pressured condition, engineers (or programmers or whoever) are induced to work on something—anything—that will demonstrate *progress* is being made. This usually translates into working more and more out of sequence, that is, on items that plans or cold logic indicate should be done later in the work sequence, when more of their prerequisites—products or information—would be available. "But surely parts of those items could be worked now [even if we aren't quite as efficient in doing them], and, why, we could even release those items [so they will add to our bean-count, even if they need to be

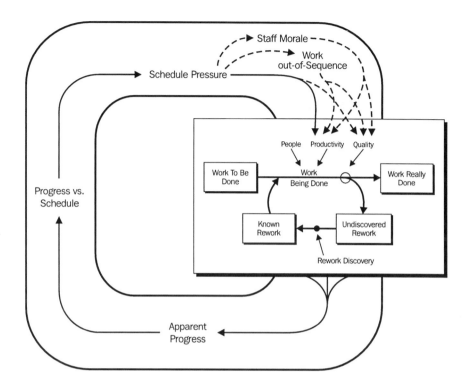

Figure 9 Paths of Influence from Schedule Pressure

reworked later]." So, with this familiar refrain, of which we are nearly all guilty, we trigger the desired short-term apparent progress gains. And we set the stage for even more trouble later when the resulting rework gets recognized.

Once more we'll add these effects, at the strengths we have seen them operate in many development projects and programs, to the simulation model. The nature of the results in Figure 10 should be no surprise. That young manager-in-training and his turn-the-screws plan, though typical, hurts final project performance far more than any temporary gain, through its unintended effects on the rework cycle.

Contrasting the results from this, our most realistic simulation of the project's performance (labeled P) with the prior simulation (labeled Q), we see a steady pattern of marginally worse conditions. The poorer performance generally does not show until the latter

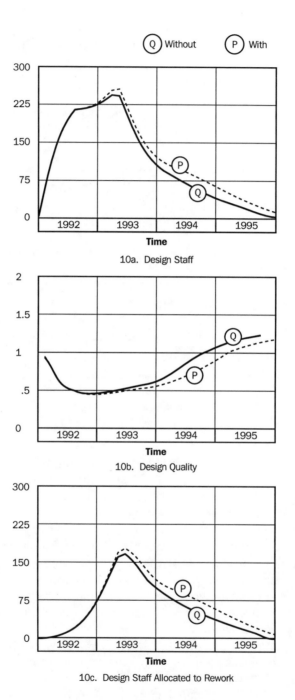

Figure 10 The Project, With the Secondary Effects of Schedule Pressure

half of the effort, as the heightened pressures tend to occur well into the project, and generate most of their impact from mid-1993 onward. The increased staffing (10a)—another 100,000 hours' worth—again stems exclusively from the adversely affected productivity (10b) and work quality (which generates more rework—10c). Together they push the second hump of staffing higher still, and extend the tail of the design effort into 1996. Rework effort now accounts for about 60 percent of the total hours spent on design, and causes the vast majority of the increase in hours spent.

And remember our old friend, overtime? The steadily eroding conditions of the program (as we have worked toward a more realistic model) have *forced* the (simulated) managers into using more and more of it—now more than twice the amount in the first simulations. And its sustained use has worsened its adverse effects, thus further contributing to the cost and schedule growth described.

Indeed, all of the previously cited effects are aggravated as the project performance has become worse (more real—part of what one of our clients has termed a *death spiral*. Being talented engineers by training, they also recognize it to be the mutually reinforcing interconnection among several *positive* feedback loops.

How far we've come. It was such an innocent-looking project at the start. Each step along the way added some more troubles and realism. The *normal* managerial responses, all aimed to exert control, brought unintended side effects and penalties through paths of influence generally not well understood, or at least underestimated.

Figure 11 helps illustrate just how far we *progressed.* We added 600,000 hours to the design effort (11a, X plots show the original conditions; P plots, the final) through productivity losses (11b) and more rework (11c). *Especially* rework—it alone increased by 500,000 hours. A plan-beating staff profile that had peaked in mid-1992 at 150 people became a serious overrun, with a second peak at 250 people a year later.

By mid-1993, when the build effort that was using the design product was under way, the original simulation displayed a perception of design readiness (see 12a in Figure 12) near 95 percent (and accounting for the undiscovered rework, really was at 75 percent—see 12b). The final, real project simulation displayed a perceived design readiness of 85 percent at the same time (12a), but much more undiscovered rework meant the design product was really only 50 percent complete (12b).

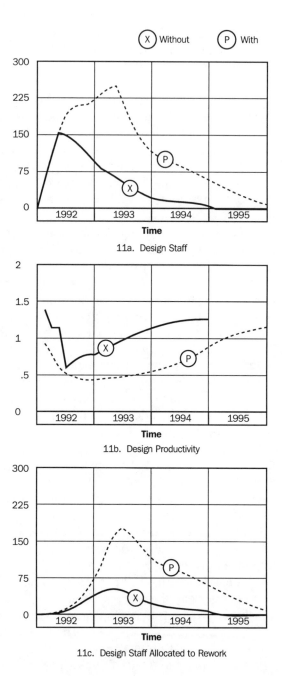

11a. Design Staff

11b. Design Productivity

11c. Design Staff Allocated to Rework

Figure 11 The Project, With and Without the Secondary Effects of Management Actions

While we've focused on the design effort, the build (construction/production) effort has been being simulated all along. And the difference between the two extreme conditions, in terms of engineering readiness and the magnitude of design changes, is enough to cause more than a doubling in build labor costs (12c—and a full year's slippage. Rather than comfortably beating the total labor cost budget of $50 million, the project incurs over $110 million in direct labor costs.[13]

It Works Both Ways

What are we as managers, executives, and customers to do? Move to a world where the undesired secondary influences don't occur? Sadly, that world exists only in unrealistic models and the minds of some managers (and executives and customers).

Or should we exercise restraint in some of the *standard* managerial responses of sustained overtime, extensive hiring, rapid staffing in the face of incomplete prerequisites—even under the pressure to *show progress*—and *turning the screws on the staff*? As an indication of just how much improvement is possible, we used the *same* fully operating model of the *same* project to test the results of just such a policy of restraint. In doing so, we are, in effect, causing the many paths of influence described earlier to work *for* us—less overtime, less productivity reduction from fatigue, less rapid hiring, more experience, less rework, judicious early staffing, less knock-on quality impact, lower pressures, better morale, higher productivity, and so on.

The results are displayed in Figure 13 (labeled with M). The slower staff build-up, though still peaking in mid-1993 (13a), does so at a level substantially below that of the prior project conditions (labeled P) on which the new simulation builds. And while the apparent completion seems every bit as slow at first (13b), we finish sooner, and achieve higher levels of *real* completion throughout (13c). The improvements achieved are, of course, a result of toning down the undesired impacts on productivity, which is better from start to finish (13d), and *much* less rework (13e). In fact, we manage to cut rework effort down nearly to half its former magnitude. That alone saves 250,000 engineering hours, and another 125,000 hours are saved by higher productivity. This total reduction of 375,000 hours is a saving of over 35 percent *and* allows us to finish seven months earlier.

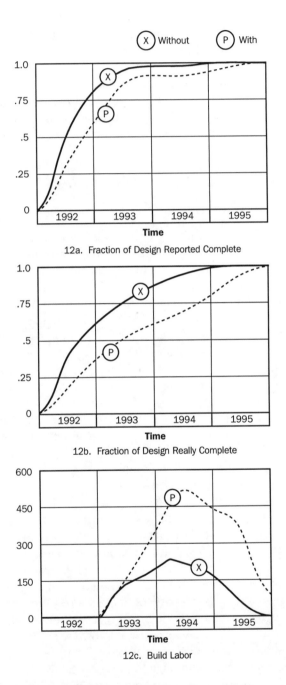

12a. Fraction of Design Reported Complete

12b. Fraction of Design Really Complete

12c. Build Labor

Figure 12 More About the Project, With and Without the Secondary Effects of Management Actions

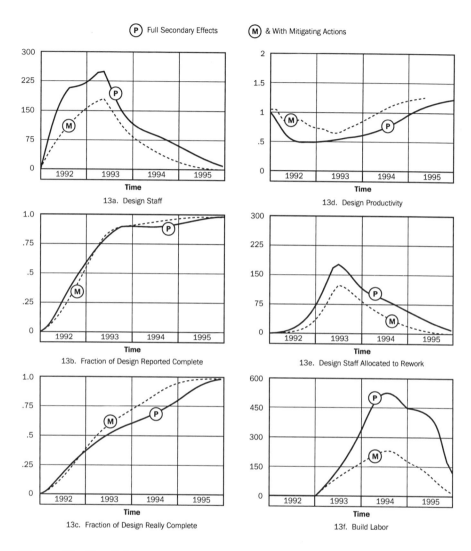

Figure 13 The Full Project, With and Without Improved Management

In improving design conditions so much, we avoid most of the adverse effects that were causing productivity and rework problems in *production*, saving over a million hours and nearly a full year in the accompanying build effort (13f). All this despite (or rather, because of) less overtime, restrained hiring, some intermediate slippage of early schedule milestones, and lessened pressures.

The bar chart in Figure 14 summarizes the project's cost and schedule performance throughout the sequence of simulations. With the implementation of the changed management policies comes dramatic improvement. Total savings: almost a full year on the schedule, and $50 million, within striking distance of the original budget.

Is this for real? Although the numbers and plots shown here were produced by a simulation model, that model is in fact of a real development program, with the numbers and time frame changed modestly to disguise its identity. The simulated conditions and performance have been carefully validated to portray the real conditions and performance, and managers have used the results for diagnosing and supporting real multimillion-dollar decisions.

But is it just one aberrant, albeit real, program? Three points suggest otherwise—indeed, that it is typical rather than aberrant. First, the disguising numerical modifications we made only moved the performance toward the *average of several dozen modeled programs*. Second, in those dozens, every single program has displayed at least three of the four *secondary* phenomena discussed here.

Finally, there is the nonanalytical, nonstatistical test of common sense and experience. If you are a veteran of one or more difficult programs, take a few moments to recall your own experience, and ask yourself how consistently you observed, or can look back and discern, those phenomena at work on your programs and projects. Recognizing them is an important step; understanding the cause-effect paths through which they work, another. Being able to simulate their performance is sometimes helpful, but it is only one means to help people take the difficult final step of acting (be it as manager, executive, or customer) to mitigate the secondary effects on productivity and quality in the rework cycles of your programs.

CONCLUSION

Projects are composed not of individual discrete tasks, but of *flows* of work, much of which will cycle to be reworked. Managers can and do strongly influence the performance of the rework cycle, and thereby the project's cost and schedule. This influence moves through paths of cause and effect, generating often unintended, usually undesired, impacts on worker productivity and work quality. Examples include

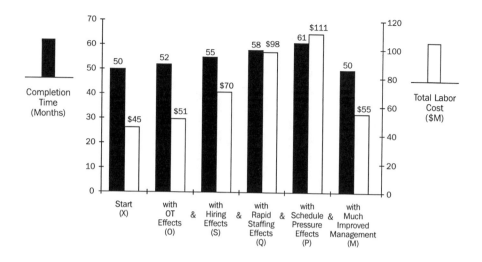

Figure 14 Project Cost and Schedule Performance Summary

the sustained use of overtime, rapid hiring, and exerting conflicting pressures on project staff. Such paths of influence can *close on themselves* to form self-reinforcing vicious circles that cause degenerative conditions.

Further, these circular paths, or feedback loops, interact with one another to compound each other's effects. In this way projects too consistently move from honeymoon to trouble to *out of control.* By understanding the paths of influence, and where in each path we as managers can exert influence, we can achieve enormous leverage on the project by changing the performance of the rework cycle. The problem is that once we have that understanding, the implied action (or restraint) is often in career-threatening opposition to *conventional wisdom.*

If programs and projects were models, the difficult advice offered herein could be easily implemented, the results examined, and lessons learned and transferred. Instead, programs and projects involve a high-stakes complex of technical, organizational, financial, personal, and political interactions. For a manager to adopt a stance that is counter to the traditional accepted thinking and the accompanying pressures requires insight. Maintaining the stance requires healthy doses of courage and leadership.

As executives, we can establish a company environment for projects that does not discourage—perhaps even helps—such management, without second-guessing. As customers, we can show more restraint in the understandable inclinations to inject mid-stream technical change and to micro-manage contractors if we understand just how disruptive to our programs those actions are. Without this better understanding among all key players, we condemn ourselves to repeating in the future the long history of important projects that badly overrun cost and schedule targets, foster costly and divisive disputes, and threaten our competitiveness.

Notes

1. Dr. Edward B. Roberts. December 10, 1992. Strategic Management of Technology: Global Benchmarking. Results of a survey sponsored and conducted by the Massachusetts Institute of Technology, Cambridge, Massachusetts, and PA Consulting.
2. Flops. August 16, 1993. *Business Week.*
3. A misnomer: Such systems control nothing; they monitor costs and progress, and often do not do that too well. See "The Rework Cycle: Benchmarks for the Project Manager," Cooper, K. G., *Project Management Journal*, March 1993.
4. The scale for productivity is in terms of work products (e.g., drawings) per person year.
5. 12 hours x $50/hour x 1.5 overtime premium = $900; $900/0.4 output hour = $2,250 per output hour. Use your own company's wage rates and overtime pay premium to calculate your projects' real overtime output costs.
6. The most recent analysis we found elsewhere; a November 1980 report of a Construction Industry Cost Effectiveness Task Force, "Scheduled Overtime Effect on Construction Projects," published by *The Business Roundtable*, showed similar, even some more extreme, phenomena among construction workers. Interestingly, the same crossover point, ten hours weekly overtime (sustained for two months), was identified as yielding no extra real output; more overtime than that produces less than a standard workweek.
7. *The Mythical Man-Month: Essays on Software Engineering.* Frederick J. Brooks. 1975. University of North Carolina, Chapel Hill.
8. Vicious circle, indeed! This even qualifies as an evil ellipse.
9. Better to have a good working analog watch—with just the hour hand! We offered Progress Ramps as approximately accurate translators of monitored progress in "The Rework Cycle: Benchmarks for the Project Manager," *Project Management Journal*, March 1993.

10. Literally, the word *reserved*, or a similar notation on the diagram or document.
11. The *quality* measure displayed here is the fraction of the work then being done that will not require subsequent rework.
12. Besides, remember the undesirable consequences already described for rapid or large increases in staffing.
13. And this does not count the added costs of any *marching army*—i.e., *support* staff incurring more expenditures as such level-of-effort functions are continued for a longer time—nor does it count any increased unit costs for another year of inflation.

Critical Success Factors across the Project Life Cycle

Jeffrey K. Pinto, College of Business Administration, University of Cincinnati
Dennis P. Slevin, Graduate School of Business, University of Pittsburgh

Project Management Journal (June 1988)

ATTEMPTS TO UNDERSTAND the process of project manage ment, involving the successful implementation of projects in organizations, represent a problem of continual concern and interest to both researchers and project managers. Much has been written to assist project managers in their efforts to more effectively manage and guide a variety of organizational projects. Both empirical and conceptual approaches have been applied to the study of the project implementation process. As a result, a wide range of critical factors or project dynamics has been uncovered, which has been found to significantly contribute to project success (e.g., sufficient available resources or top management support). While these findings have had an important impact on project managers, helping them to better manage their projects to completion, few researches have attempted to determine how the *importance* of these critical factors may fluctuate as a result of changes in the life cycle of the project. In other words, it may be likely that some *critical* factors may become more or less critical to project success, depending upon the phase in its life cycle that the project currently occupies.

The purpose of this article is to report on the results of a recent study conducted in an effort to test the importance of those factors that have long been believed to be critical to project success. Over six hundred questionnaires were mailed to project managers and members of the Project Management Institute (PMI). The response rate and interest level generated from this study have been quite strong; over four hundred questionnaires were returned, indicating a response rate in excess of 71 percent.

Specifically, this study resulted in two important findings, as follows.

1. The validation of a set of factors previously discovered as critical to project implementation success (Slevin and Pinto 1986).

2. The determination that these factors are not of equal and stable importance over the life of the project. Rather, different sets of these factors become more critical to project success at different phases in the project life cycle.

The results of this study have important implications for project managers and researchers in the project management field. First, a set of ten critical success factors were determined that improve the prediction of project implementation success. Second, this study demonstrates that it is insufficient to simply ask the question, "Which factors are most important to project success?" It will be shown using project life cycles that the relative importance of various critical factors is subject to dramatic changes at different phases in the project implementation process. Finally, this research offers support for use of the project implementation profile (PIP) (Slevin and Pinto 1986) as an instrument to assess project performance and predict project success based on responses across the ten critical factors.

PROJECT CRITICAL SUCCESS FACTORS

Research in the area of critical success factors in project management and implementation has been conducted for several years. Many examples exist of both empirical studies aimed at determining critical success factors (Baker et al. 1983; Thamhain and Wilemon 1986), as well as conceptual research approaches (Cleland and King 1983; Archibald 1976; Locke 1984) that have developed theoretical frameworks or models listing several of those factors seen as critical to project success.

Recent work by Slevin and Pinto (1986; 1987) has led to both the development of a ten-factor model of the project implementation process and an instrument that may be used to empirically monitor the current state of each of the ten critical factors throughout a project's life. These ten characteristics represent those attributes found to be critical to project implementation success. (For a more in-depth discussion of how these factors were developed and some of the important considerations included within each of the factors, see Slevin and Pinto, 1986). The ten critical success factors can be briefly defined as follows.

1. Project mission—initial clarity of goals and general directions.

2. Top management support—willingness of top management to provide the necessary resources and authority/power for project success.

3. Project schedule/plans—a detailed specification of the individual action steps required for project implementation.

4. Client consultation—communication, consultation, and active listening to all impacted parties.

5. Personnel—recruitment, selection, and training of the necessary personnel for the project team.

6. Technical tasks—availability of the required technology and expertise to accomplish the specific technical action steps.

7. Client acceptance—the act of *selling* the final project to its ultimate intended users.

8. Monitoring and feedback—timely provision of comprehensive control information at each phase in the implementation process.

9. Communication—the provision of an appropriate network and necessary data to all key factors in the project implementation

10. Troubleshooting—ability to handle unexpected crises and deviations from plan.

In addition to these ten critical success factors, all of which to some degree are within the control of the project team, four additional factors were included in this study. Both research and interviews with a variety of project managers have suggested the importance of these factors for project success. These factors represent critical areas or issues that are often considered *beyond the control* of the project team, but which nevertheless are felt to have an important impact on project success. The four factors are labeled as external to the project implementation process and can be defined as follows.

1. Characteristics of the project team leader—competence of the project leader (administratively, interpersonally, and technically) and the amount of authority available to perform her duties.

2. Power and politics—the degree of political activity within the organization and perception of the project as furthering an organization member's self-interests.

3. Environmental events—the likelihood of external organizational or environmental factors impacting on the operations of the project team, either positively or negatively.

4. Urgency—the perception of the importance of the project or the need to implement the project as soon as possible.

THE PROJECT LIFE CYCLE

The use of life cycles in project management is not a new concept to most project managers. Much has been written on the use of life-cycle analysis and its impact on project management (Adams and Barndt 1983; King and Cleland 1983). Life cycles have been used to explain the impact of a variety of behavioral issues on the project organization. For example, studies have examined propensity toward conflict and effective conflict management styles at different phases in the life cycle (Thamhain and Wilemon 1975). Other research has argued that the leadership styles of the project manager must change at different phases in the project life cycle (Adams and Barndt 1983). These and other authors have presented a strong case for the inclusion of the project life-cycle phase into investigations of the dynamics of the project implementation process.

In this study, a four-phase life cycle has been employed (see Figure 1). The initial phase, *conceptualization*, refers to the point at which a strategic need has been recognized by top management. Typically, preliminary goals and alternatives for the project are established at this point, along with exploring the availability of the means (resources) to accomplish these goals. Conceptualization often involves an initial feasibility decision requiring that management answer questions, such as the following.

- What is the problem?
- Will the development of a project solve that problem?
- What are the specific goals of the project?
- Do we have the resources to create and support the project?

The second phase in the project life cycle is referred to as the *planning* phase. In this phase, once top management has given the *go ahead* to launch the project, a more formalized set of plans to accomplish the initially developed goals is established. Some of the

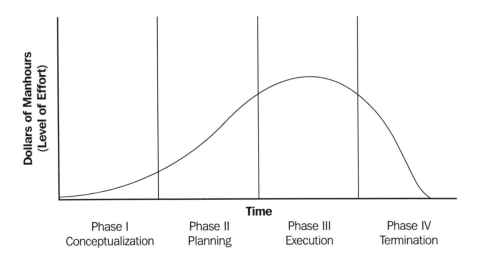

Figure 1 Phases in the Project Life Cycle

well-known planning functions are determining the availability of needed resources, budgeting, and the allocation of specific tasks.

The third phase is labeled *execution*. It is during the execution phase that the actual *work* of the project is performed. Sufficient materials and resources are procured and transformed into the intended project result. During this phase, performance capabilities are continually tested to ensure that the project performs as intended.

The fourth and final phase in the project life cycle is called the *termination* phase. Once the project has been completed, the project team is often disbanded, and personnel are reassigned to other duties; resources that were secured for the project are now released back to the parent organization, and the project is transferred to its intended users.

As Figure 1 shows, in addition to demonstrating the four distinct phases in the project life cycle, the model also specifies the level of organizational effort (resources, man-hours, and so forth) necessary to adequately perform the tasks associated with each project phase. As one would expect, during the early conceptualization and planning phases, resource and effort requirement are often minimal, increasing rapidly during late planning and execution before diminishing again in the project's termination. As a result, the concept of project life cycles is useful for project managers, not only through distinguishing among distinct phases in the project's life, but also through indicating likely resource requirements associated with each project phase.

This study was conducted to show the added impact that project life cycles can have on critical success factors. It was argued that different sets of these factors should be found to be more or less critical to project success, depending upon the current phase in the project life cycle. The focus of our research was to test this idea.

THE STUDY

The data sample. Questionnaires were mailed to over six hundred members of t he Project Management Institute—a national organization of project managers. Due to terminations, retirements, and other reasons, a total of 586 project managers were capable of responding to the questionnaire, of which 418 were usable, resulting in a response rate exceeding 71 percent. This response rate was three to five times the national norm for mail surveys, indicating the considerable interest of this topic to project managers.

Three types of questionnaires were randomly mailed to the sample group. One questionnaire asked the respondents to think of a *successful* project in which they were currently involved or had recently completed. The second questionnaire asked the subjects to consider an *unsuccessful* project with which they had experience. The third questionnaire did not specify the type of project for them to consider. Three types of questionnaires were used to ensure a wide sample of projects, both in terms of phase of project completion and final outcome (successes and failures).

Table 1 shows the distribution of projects in the sample. Although there was a wide cross section of projects represented, construction projects made up 44 percent of the sample. The industries represented in the sample were from the manufacturing as well as service sectors and included a mixture from the public and private domains. Projects included in the sample ranged from a $5,000 test study conducted in a small firm to a $2 billion government-funded research project.

Table 2 shows the breakdown of respondents to the questionnaire by the position they occupy. Not surprisingly, the majority

Type	Absolute Frequency Percentage	Relative Frequency Percentage	Cumulative Frequency
Construction	185	44.3	44.3
Hardware, Equipment, or Appliance Development	40	9.6	53.9
Food, Drug, or Soft Goods Development	58	13.9	67.8
New or Improved Software Development	61	14.6	82.4
Service or Test	12	2.9	85.3
Study	13	3.1	88.4
Departmental Reorganization or Move to New Facility	17	4.1	92.5
Miscellaneous	32	7.5	100.0
Total	418		

Table 1 Frequency Distributions on Type of Project

(50.2 percent) of those responding to the questionnaire were project managers. However, a significant percentage of responses came from other members of the project team, including administrators, technical personnel, and others. This diversity of respondents indicates that the data sample represented a wide range of perspectives.

Before completing the questionnaire, each respondent was asked to think of a project in which he was involved that was currently under way or recently completed. This project was to be his frame of reference while completing the questionnaire. The four-phase project-life-cycle model discussed earlier was included in the questionnaire and was used to identify the current phase of each project.

Table 3 shows the breakdown of responses by project phase. As can be seen, thirty-six (8.6 percent) of the responses were based on projects in the conceptual phase. Seventy-three (17.5 percent) of the projects reported on were in the planning phase, 202 (48.3 percent)

Role	Absolute Frequency Percentage	Relative Frequency Percentage	Cumulative Frequency
Project Manager	210	50.2	50.2
Manager on Project Team	55	13.2	63.4
Project Team Member —Technical	25	5.9	69.3
Project Team Member —Administrative	57	13.6	82.9
Member of Business Unit Affected by Project	11	2.6	85.5
Other	60	14.5	100.0
Total	418		

Table 2 Frequency Distributions on Position of Respondent

of the projects were in the execution phase, and 107 (25.6 percent) were undergoing project termination.

QUESTIONNAIRE

The project implementation profile (PIP) was used to identify critical success factors and subsequent factor scores over the project life cycle. The PIP requires participants to indicate their levels of agreement on a seven-point scale to a series of seventy-two questions, covering the ten critical factors and four additional external factors felt to be related to project implementation success. The seven-point scale required responses ranging from Strongly Agree to Strongly Disagree for each item.

Project success. The PIP's measure of project success is an average of thirteen items comprising assessments of adherence to budget and schedule, project performance capabilities, technical validity, organizational validity, and organizational effectiveness. The measure of

Phase	Absolute Frequency Percentage	Relative Frequency Percentage	Cumulative Frequency
Conceptual	36	8.6	8.6
Planning	73	17.5	26.1
Execution	202	48.3	74.4
Termination	<u>107</u>	25.6	100.0
Total	418		

Table 3 Frequency Distributions on Phase of Project

success was specifically constructed to be multidimensional in an effort to include, as nearly as possible, all aspects associated with project implementation success.

Traditionally, there has been general agreement that any assessment of project success must include measures of budgetary and schedule adherence, as well as the confirmation of performance capabilities. In addition, it has been suggested that in order for the project to be considered successful, it must be technically valid. In other words, the project must work, and it must be a technically correct solution to the problem for which the project was initiated (Schultz and Slevin 1975). Furthermore, the project must be organizationally valid. In other words, the project to be implemented must *fit* the organization or clients for whom it is intended, and they must make use of it. Finally, the project to be implemented should result in some form of improved level of organizational effectiveness or decision-making (Schultz and Slevin 1979). The client's organization should be assessed as being more *effective* as a result of the implemented project. To summarize, project success was measured based on the following characteristics:

- adherence to budget
- adherence to schedule
- level of performance achieved
- technical validity
- organizational validity
- organizational effectiveness.

Variable	Beta	T	Sig. T
Project Mission	.72	19.99	p < .01
Top Management Support	.32	10.60	p < .01
Schedule/Plans	.32	10.92	p < .01
Client Consultation	.39	11.86	p < .01
Personnel	.31	10.54	p < .01
Technical Tasks	.43	11.25	p < .01
Client Acceptance	.39	11.46	p < .01
Monitoring and Feedback	.29	10.89	p < .01
Communication	.32	10.38	p < .01
Troubleshooting	.35	11.15	p < .01
Leadership	.43	12.44	p < .01
Power and Politics	.11	3.71	p < .01
Environmental Effects	.15	4.52	p < .01
Urgency	.32	7.18	p < .01

Table 4 Regression Results of Ability of Each Critical Factor to Predict Project Success

RESULTS

As previously stated, the first objective of this study was to provide empirical evidence that the set of ten critical success factors was significantly related to project success. In addition to the ten critical factors, the four external factors (characteristics of the project team leader, power and politics, and so forth) were also evaluated to determine if they had any ability to predict project success.

The ability of each critical factor in predicting project implementation success is shown in Table 4. Each of the critical factors was tested independently against project success. As can be seen from Table 4, all fourteen of the critical factors that were used in the study were shown to be significantly related to project success. Both the beta value and the T-statistic represent the strength of the relationship that exists between each critical factor and project success. As a result, one of the first conclusions from this study is that the *ten critical success factors and the four external factors were shown to each be predictive of project success.* Further, the table indicates that the most significant relationships (most important individual factors) among the variables were between success and project mission, characteristics of the project team leader, technical tasks, client consultation, and client acceptance.

Because a second key purpose of this research was to test the *relative* stability of the critical factors across the project life cycle, a second analysis was performed. In this test, the fourteen factors were not examined individually. Rather, all fourteen variables were tested simultaneously at each of the four project life-cycle phases to determine which of the set were most important at each project phase. For each project phase, a stepwise regression technique tested all fourteen variables and initially selected the single variable that was most important in predicting project success. At the next *step*, the computer selected the second most important variable. This process continued until all variables were included, in order of importance, or until only those factors that were significant were included.

Table 5 shows the results of the stepwise regression across the four project life-cycle phases. In the conceptual phase, project mission and client consultation were the two key factors related to project success, with an adjusted r-square value of .64. In other words, at the conceptual phase in a project, two factors (project mission and client consultation) are capable of predicting 64 percent of the causes of project success. In the planning phase, project mission, top management support, client acceptance, and urgency were the key factors explaining 65 percent of the reasons for project success. For the execution phase, project mission, characteristics of the project team leader, troubleshooting, project schedule/plans, technical tasks, and client consultation together accounted for 66 percent of the causes of project success. Finally, at the phase of project termination, technical tasks, project mission, and client consultation had an r-square value of .60.

Phase 1: Conceptualization
- Project Mission
- Client Consultation

Action implications for the project manager:
- Insist on a clearly specified and on-target project mission.
- Consult with your important clients at the very outset of the project life cycle.

Stage of Project Life Cycle	Number of Projects	Factors	Adjusted ΔR²	Adjusted R²	Sig. R²
Conceptual	36	Mission	.57	.57	p < .01
		Client Consultation	.07	.64	p < .01
Planning	73	Mission	.55	.55	p < .01
		Top Mgmt. Support	.06	.61	p < .01
		Client Acceptance	.02	.63	p < .01
		Urgency	.02	.65	p < .01
Execution	202	Mission	.50	.50	p < .01
		Leadership	.06	.56	p < .01
		Troubleshooting	.05	.61	p < .01
		Schedule/Plans	.02	.63	p < .01
		Technical Tasks	.01	.65	p < .01
		Client Consultation	.01	.66	p < .01
Termination	107	Technical Tasks	.45	.45	p < .01
		Mission	.12	.57	p < .01
		Client Consultation	.03	.60	p < .01

Table 5   Key Factors for Each Phase of the Project Life Cycle from Stepwise Regression Analysis

Phase 2: Planning

- Project Mission
- Top Management Support
- Client Acceptance
- Urgency

   Action implications for the project manager:

- Continue to refine and specify the project mission—stay on target.
- Insist on top management support in terms of resources and authority.
- Go beyond client consultation and address the important issue of client acceptance. What actions can we take to help sell our ideas to the clients?
- Create a perceived sense of urgency for the project in the parent organization and among the project team members.

Phase 3: Execution

- Project Mission
- Characteristics of the Project Team Leader
- Troubleshooting
- Project Schedule/Plans
- Technical Tasks
- Client consultation

Action implications for the project manager:

- Continue to look back to the project mission for direction. Make sure you and your project team are staying on target.
- Use good management skills as the project leader. Although these characteristics may seem to be somewhat inherent and unchangeable, the use of effective management training and appropriate management tools can enhance the characteristics and skills of any project manager.
- Start the troubleshooting process at this phase. Now that you have actually started the project execution, you must have procedures for detecting and correcting the errors that crop up.
- Develop and adhere to a comprehensive schedule and/or set of plans for the implementation. You might even consider the use of project management software at this phase to keep all of the items in control.
- Initiate the execution of the technical tasks. Make sure that you have quality technical experts and adequate technology to support the project.
- Don't forget the client. Maintain an effective two-way communication flow with the user.

Phase 4: Termination

- Technical Tasks
- Project Mission
- Client Consultation

Action implications for the project manager:

- As you terminate the project, make sure that the technical system is fine-tuned and working at maximum effectiveness.
- Even at this phase, don't forget the project mission (why this mission developed). Are there any changes that you could make in this final phase to make sure that the project stays on target?
- Stay close to the client and try to make sure that you have a satisfied project user before you leave for good.

PHASES

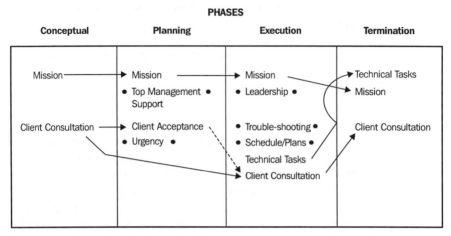

Critical Success Factors (In order of importance)

Figure 2   Summary of Study Results: Critical Factors at Each Project Phase

IMPLICATIONS FOR PROJECT MANAGERS

As one can see, a general pattern emerges from these research results that would be useful for the project manager over a broad range of projects.

1. Don't forget the project mission. The first finding relates to the importance of the factor *project mission* across all four stages in the project life cycle. Intuitively, it is not surprising that the mission should have an important impact on project success; particularly early in the project's life. What is surprising, however, is that a focus on the project mission continues to remain of great importance throughout the implementation of the project. This result suggests the need to always keep the goals and purposes of the project being implemented in the forefront. Further, the purpose of and goals for the project need to be made evident, not only to a few select members of the project team, but also to all project team members. A large proportion of those responding to this study were not project managers, but were team members of varying levels. These respondents also indicated the importance of project mission at all life-cycle phases. An effective management strategy is to continually emphasize the *purpose* of the project to all team members, keeping the goals in focus throughout the life of the project.

2. Client consultation: Keep the channels open. A second interesting finding is the importance of interaction with the project's clients throughout the life of the project. Client consultation—a communicating, listening, and feedback activity—was very important at three of the four life-cycle states: conceptualization, execution, and termination. Client acceptance—a *selling* function—was of prime importance during the planning phase. A possible conclusion drawn from these results would be that the project team must first listen and ask questions; next, sell its ideas, project capabilities, and time frame to completion; then engage in continuous two-way communication throughout the life of the project. As was implied previously, these results suggest that it would be a mistake for the project team to initially talk to clients and subsequently sever this connection to go off and develop the project on their own. As stated above, it is important to keep the channels open.

3. Be meticulous about schedules. As the strategic plan for the project is implemented, it is essential for the effective project manager to put together a schedule and/or set of plans for the project and use it on a regular basis. The schedule represents a highly important and necessary element to successful project execution. During the actual work of the project, the schedule often functions as the sole feedback mechanism to many project members in assessing how the project is proceeding. As a result, proper attention to schedules represents an important consideration for both project leaders and team members, not only in terms of actual time frame to completion, but also as a periodic checklist for feedback on project performance.

4. Make sure we have the technical means to succeed. Another result of this study is the determination that technical tasks are important for project success during the execution and termination phases of the project. Technical tasks argue for adequate technology and competent personnel to assist in the technical action steps of the implementation. This result, along with the finding that troubleshooting and schedule/plans were critical during the execution phase, suggests that tactical issues become more important to project success as the project progresses through its life cycle. *Tactics* implies those operational activities that are performed in support of strategic plans. While this result appears to be obvious, it needs to be considered in light of the fact that project mission, a strategy/

planning activity, is critical throughout the project's life. Project strategy and tactics must work hand in hand, particularly during execution and termination, in order to ensure greater likelihood of success.

5. Project leadership: It can make a difference. Much has been written about the important positive effects a competent leader can have on her project team and the resulting success of the project. Although the findings support these conclusions, they further suggest that project leadership becomes most important during the actual *work* or execution of the project. At this point, the various competencies of the project team leader (technical, administrative, and interpersonal) are most crucial for project success. While the project team leader will assume various roles throughout the project development (motivator, conflict resolver, *visionary*, and so forth), project team leadership can make its presence felt most during the project's execution.

6. Make the project important. A last finding from the study was the positive impact of perceived urgency or importance on project success, particularly during the planning phase. In one sense, it seems obvious to tell project managers that *important* or urgent projects have a better chance for success, but the point bears emphasizing. Not all projects run through an organization are seen as urgent, or even necessary. In spite of the pronouncements of project managers or top management, in many instances project team members perceive their project as routine, dull, or pointless. As the results point out, the perception of a project as important or unique can have strong impact on its likelihood for success. This finding is particularly true during the planning phase of the project life cycle. An implication for project managers would be to attempt to instill within the project team members a feeling that what they are engaged in has importance for them as a project team, for the parent organization, and for the clients for whom the project is intended.

CONCLUSIONS

The purpose of this article has been to report on some of the important findings resulting from a large-scale study investigating the role of specific critical factors in project implementation success. The results support much of the theoretical and empirical work that has been done to date on the role these factors play in project success. The importance of several of these critical factors to project success should not be intuitively surprising to many project managers. However, it was proven through this analysis that it is insufficient to simply ask the question, "What factors are most important to project success?" The answer was shown to depend on the *phase of the life cycle* in which the project resides. As a result, project managers are presented with empirical evidence suggesting that attention be paid to specific sets of critical factors at each of the four project life-cycle phases. These factors were shown to have a powerful impact on project success, in some cases accounting for up to 66 percent of the causes of successful project implementation.

Successful project implementation can be a difficult, complex task. The project manager is continually bombarded with a wide variety of input and information from project team members, the parent organization, and clients. The practical benefit of the research that has been reported in this article has been to help in clarifying not only the roles that a successful project manager must undertake, but also those duties which have been shown to contribute to successful project implementation. It is hoped that through focusing attention on these roles and critical factors, the project manager will be in a better position to actively monitor and steer his future projects toward successful conclusions.

References

Adams, J. R., and S. E. Brandt. 1983. Behavioral Implications of the Project Life Cycle. In *Project Management Handbook*. Eds. D. I. Cleland and W. R. King. New York: Van Nostrand Reinhold Co., 222–45.

Archibald, R. D. 1976. *Managing High-Technology Programs and Projects*. New York: John Wiley and Sons.

Baker, B. N., D. C. Murphy, and D. Fisher. 1983. Factors Affecting Project Success. In *Project Management Handbook*. Eds. D. I. Cleland and W. R. King. New York: Van Nostrand Reinhold Co., 669–85.

Cleland, D. I., and W. R. King. 1983. *Systems Analysis and Project Management*. New York: McGraw-Hill Inc.

King, W. R., and D. I. Cleland. 1983. Life Cycle Management. In *Project Management Handbook*. Eds. D. I. Cleland and W. R. King. New York: Van Nostrand Reinhold Co., 209–21.

Locke, D. 1984. *Project Management*. New York: St. Martins Press.

———. 1987. Critical Factors in Successful Project Implementation. *IEEE Transactions on Engineering Management*. EM-34.1: 22–27.

Schultz, R. L., and D. P. Slevin. 1975. Implementation and Management Innovation. *Implementing Operations Research and Management Science*. Eds. R. L. Schultz and D. P. Slevin. New York: Elsevier, 3–22.

———. 1979. Introduction: The Implementation Problem. *The Implementation of Management Science*. Ed. R. Doktor, R. L. Schultz, and D. P. Slevin. Amsterdam: North-Holland, 1–15.

Slevin, Dennis P., and Jeffrey K. Pinto. 1986. The Project Implementation Profile: New Tool for Project Management. *Project Management Journal* 27.4: 55–70.

Thamhain, H. J., and D. I. Wilemon. 1975. Conflict Management in Project Life Cycles. *Sloan Management Review* 17: 31–50.

———. 1986. Criteria for Controlling Projects According to Plan. *Project Management Journal* 27.3: 75–81.

The Case for Earned Value

Michael A. Hatfield, PMP

PM Network (Dec. 1996)

How are we doing?" For the remainder of this article, I'll refer to this question as *the* question—as critical to project management types as "What is the meaning of life?" is to philosophers and "Would you like to buy this flower?" is to airport Moonies. The ability to answer *the* question quickly and accurately is what project control theory is really all about.

Amazingly, the one most important tool used in answering *the* question has come under fire in some quarters, most notably in the government sector. The use of earned value is commonplace in private enterprise, but its government-housed cousin, the budgeted cost of work performed (BCWP), has become more unpopular at the Department of Energy and is virtually alien to projects at the Department of the Interior. Real project management types can grind their teeth in frustration all they want, but sissy project management types are doing away with this, the most important of cost management tools, in a most glacier-like fashion: slowly, coldly, and seemingly unstoppably.

When I have occasion to teach the cost section of *A Guide to the Project Management Body of Knowledge (PMBOK® Guide)*, either at the University of New Mexico or in small, in-house sessions, I like to start with a story problem, as follows.

> "You are a project manager," I begin, "and you are in charge of a two-month project." (Some will begin to write this down, while others continue to stare blankly.) "You are to make 2,000 widgets in two months, and you have a $2,000 budget to accomplish it. That works out to 1,000 widgets and $1,000 per month, right?" (Okay so far, although some are beginning to suspect they will have to think in a minute.) "At the end of the first month, you have spent $1,100." Then comes *the* question: *"How are you doing?"*
>
> The blankly staring types usually offer the first answer, because the others already suspect a trick question. "We are doing poorly. We're overspent."
>
> "So, you might go tell the shop foreman that you are disappointed with the project team's performance?"
>
> "Yeah, probably."
>
> "What if I were to tell you that you have completed 1,300 widgets?"
>
> (Silence.)

This problem illustrates, in a nutshell, the case for earned value. Simply comparing the budget with the actuals (the *accountant's folly*) tells you next to nothing. Without some assessment of how much of the project's objectives have been met in relation to how many had been planned, the difference between budget and actual costs can be misleading and produce wrong decisions, such as yelling at the widget project's shop foreman.

Another example of the irrefutably high value of earned value lies in the fact that *even those project managers who refuse to do it formally will do it informally*. Which project manager, upon hearing that she has spent half of her budget, does not automatically think, "Am I half done?"

Of course, private-sector managers rarely need to be convinced of the importance of earned value. In eleven years as a management consultant, the best earned-value-based management information system I have seen was not at the departments of defense or energy or in government at all. Levi Strauss' Albuquerque plant had a remarkable system in place, generating a report that resembled a cost performance report (format 1) *every hour*. A quantity of denim would arrive at the loading dock with a ticket describing the number and style of garment that was expected. Each machine used in processing the garments kept track of actual costs and time, as well as the number of garments that had been processed and to what extent they had been finished.

Tight variance thresholds allowed true management-by-exception, as negative variances attracted the attention of floor supervisors, who could help the operators or assign extra personnel. Positive variances were noted in individual employee records and served as the basis for bonuses.

The earned value information that was being collected and used as the basis for the needed management information was so ingrained in the way this plant did its business that the Levi Strauss managers and floor supervisors literally could not imagine doing business without their hourly status reports.

If earned value is so critical to the way business should be done, then why the controversy in the public sector? One of the biggest reasons has to do with management philosophy. Traditional management approaches are rooted in the financial manager's life goal: maximize shareholder earnings. It is obvious that making decisions that save the shareholders' money will help achieve this goal—what is not so obvious is that achieving customer satisfaction helps achieve this goal as well. Making management decisions based on the make-the-customer-happy approach are often in conflict with *short-term* moneymaking (or saving) tactics, and it takes a farsighted manager to recognize the inherent tradeoff in such decisions. Earned value is a critical performance indicator, meaning that it belongs in the realm of the meeting-customer-objectives approach.

In other words, the importance of earned value as a tool is rarely obvious to traditional management philosophy types. True project managers, however, have learned that they cannot manage a project of any size without it. To them, there is no cost management without earned value.

Also contributing to this management tool's unpopularity is an unfortunate but commonly held notion that management, like leadership, is next to impossible to learn—that you either have it or you do not. To many managers, the ability to manage should be somewhat intuitive, and should certainly not require any education past common sense. Hydro-geologists adopting such an approach are called *dowsers*, and surgeons embracing this approach are denigrated as *witch doctors*.

Managers with this approach (no, they are not called *vice presidents*) are just as dangerous, because many projects conducted by the government and its contractors have serious, widespread effects. I am not saying that any manager that does not use earned value is ignorant or superstitious; but they are certainly less informed than their BCWP-using counterparts.

The next-to-last point I will make is that I have never heard a valid argument against the use of earned value. That is not to say that I have never heard criticisms and complaints about it. People say it is too complicated (it is not), that it is hard to implement (not really), that their project is too small to benefit from it (this occurs but rarely), or that they will not benefit from the reports (this guy is a *project manager*?).

Finally, what project management tool is there to replace it? Imagine a carpenter who disliked the carpenter's square. Clearly, he would need a tool that performs this function, or else his work would become crooked rather quickly. Project managers who eschew earned value should consider if the tool they use in its place is sufficient, or if their management has become as poor as the square-less carpenter's.

So, how *are* you doing?

Implementing Earned Value Easily and Effectively

Daniel M. Brandon, Jr., School of Business, Christian Brothers University

Project Management Journal 29.2 (June 1998)

EARNED VALUE IS a quantitative approach to evaluating true performance of a project both in terms of cost deviation and schedule deviation. It also provides a quantitative basis for estimating actual completion time and actual cost at completion. However, the effective use of this important technique is relatively rare outside of the United States government and its contractors (Fleming and Koppleman 1996). Earned value is one of the most underused cost management tools available to project managers (Fleming and Koppleman 1994). There are several reasons for this lack of use, and these reasons involve the overcomplication of the surrounding methodology and procedures, and also the effort and human factors involved in gathering the necessary input data, and reporting and integrating the results with other management information systems. This paper presents some methodologies that when integrated into the basic earned value approach will yield a simple yet very effective quantitative project management tool.

EARNED VALUE HISTORY

The earned value concept has been around in several forms for many years, dating back to types of cost variances defined in the 1950s. In the early 1960s, program evaluation review technique

(PERT) was extended to include cost variances, and the basic concept of earned value was adopted therein. PERT did not survive, but the basic earned value concept did. That concept was a key element in the 1967 Department of Defense (DoD) policy, to which contractors had to comply (for contracts where the government had some or all of the risk for cost overruns), called cost/schedule control systems criteria (C/SCSC). These criteria were compiled by the Air Force in the early 1960s, and comprised thirty-five statements defining minimum requirements of an acceptable project management system. Despite these mandates, the C/SCSC requirements were typically implemented by companies in word only and not in spirit. The methodology was viewed as excessive *bean counting* rather than a true management tool; this, in part, due to excessive checklists and other paperwork, specialist acronyms, and overly complicated methods and tools. Horror stories of excessive administrative cost due to overimplementation of C/SCSC were common. However, C/SCSC has been very effective overall, and the government has accumulated years of statistical evidence supporting it. Also in the last several years, initiatives within DoD have been started to remove excessive and ineffective components of the C/SCSC (Abba 1997), and earned value is being used for in-house government projects (Hewitt and O Connor 1993) and some commercial systems (Horan and McNichols 1990).

EARNED VALUE DEFINITION

Earned value is basically the value (usually expressed in dollars) of the work accomplished up to a point in time *based upon the planned (or budgeted) value* for that work. The governments term for earned value is *budgeted cost of work performed* (BCWP).

Typically, when a schedule is being formulated, the work to be done is broken down into tasks or work packets that are organized into a logical pattern, usually called a work breakdown structure (WBS). The WBS is usually formulated in a hierarchical manner, shown for our example project in Figure 1, which has two levels.

Each work packet is assigned to an organization for work management/responsibility. The organizational structure may also be represented in a hierarchical manner, typically called an organizational breakdown structure (OBS). The amount and type of cost to complete each work packet is then estimated. Resources to perform

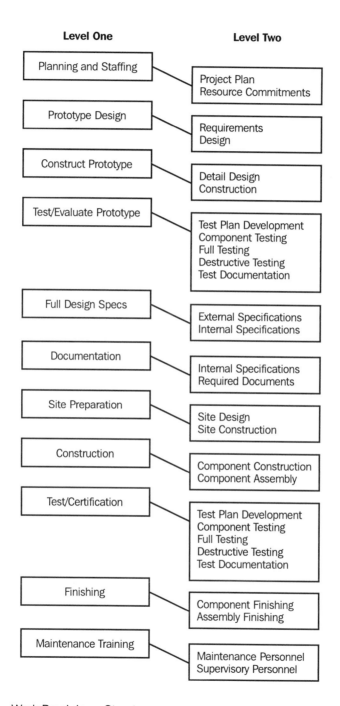

Figure 1 Work Breakdown Structure

Project Cost Plan

	Jan	Feb	Mar	Apr	May	Jun	Jul	Aug	Sep	Oct	Nov	Dec	Total
Planning and Staffing	3	2											5
Prototype Design		3	3										6
Construct Prototype			8	8									16
Test/Evaluate Prototype				5	10								15
Full Design Specs					5	6	3						14
Documentation						2	2	1	1	1	1		8
Site Preparation						8	3	3					14
Construction							20	50	50	20			140
Test/Certification								10	6	4			20
Finishing											8	4	12
Maintenance Training												4	4
Monthly Cost	3	5	11	13	15	16	28	54	61	27	13	8	254
Cumulative	3	8	19	32	47	63	91	145	206	233	246	254	

Table 1 Project Cost Plan Spreadsheet

the work are identified for each packet and may be coded by using a resource breakdown structure (RBS). Each packet typically has one type of cost (labor, travel, materials, and so on), coded by an element of cost breakdown or simple general-ledger account number. Thus, each work packet is the intersection of these coding dimensions, and it has a detailed description plus definition of WBS identification, OBS identification, RBS, element of cost, estimated cost, and dependent tasks. The estimated cost may be a function of the resources, and the dependent tasks describe a list of tasks that must be completed before starting this task. These tasks are then typically input into a scheduling program that produces a time phasing of task start and end dates based upon project start date, task resource needs, resource availability, and task interdependencies. When these tasks are *rolled up* in the WBS hierarchy, the total cost plan is derived as shown in Table 1 in spreadsheet form (for our example project) or as Figure 2 in graphical form. The government's term for this planned cost curve is *budgeted cost of work scheduled* (BCWS). With a full spreadsheet model, there would be a subsidiary spreadsheet for each Level 1 task (similar to Table 2), or for our example here, a workbook (file) of twelve spreadsheets (worksheets).

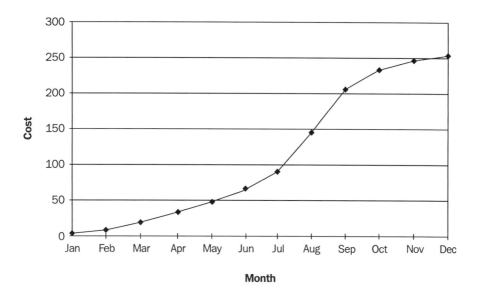

Figure 2   Project Cost Plan Graph

As the project progresses, actual costs are incurred by the effort expended in each work packet. It is hoped that these actual costs are measurable, at least in total, as shown in Figure 3. The costs may or may not be practically measurable for each work packet, which are at the lowest level of the WBS. (This is discussed later in the article.) However, the relative amount of the things needed to be accomplished within the work packet that have actually been completed (percent complete) can be estimated. The planned cost may change in time also, and thus work packets may need to be reestimated, or new ones added or deleted.

Since percent complete and earned value can be estimated for each work packet, the total project earned value at a point in time can be determined by a WBS rollup of the values. For example, if a packet had an estimated total cost of $10,000, and if the things to be done in the packet were 70 percent complete (or 70 percent of the things were complete), then the earned value would be $7,000. A WBS rollup example is shown in Table 2. There are usually *level-of-effort* (or indirect or allocated) costs associated with a project. For earned value analysis, these can be left out, or their associated work packets can be assigned 100 percent complete.

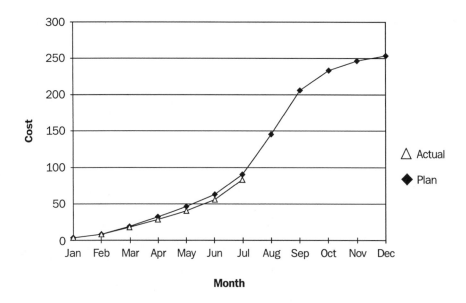

Figure 3   Plan and Actual Cost Graph

The earned value is a point on the planned cost (BCWS) curve. This is illustrated in Figure 4, which shows the planned cost and actual cost curves for a project analysis on our sample project through July. Variances between the three values—BCWS (planned cost), BCWP (earned value), and actual cost (ACWP)—yield the earned value metrics. There are earned value metrics available for both cost and schedule variances. The cost metrics include:

- Cost Variance (Dollars) = ACWP – BCWP
- Cost Variance (Percent) = (ACWP – BCWP) * 100/BCWP
- Cost Efficiency Factor = BCWP/ACWP
- Estimated Cost to Complete (EAC) = BCWS/(Cost Efficiency Factor).

There are several other EAC formulas, and the most appropriate depends upon project type and when the EAC is calculated (Horan and McNickols 1990). The schedule metrics include:

- Schedule Variance (Dollars) = BCWS – BCWP
- Schedule Variance (Months) = (BCWS – BCWP)/(Planned Cost for Month)
- Schedule Efficiency Factor = BCWP/BCWS
- Estimated Time to Complete = (Planned Completion in Months)/ (Schedule Efficiency Factor).

Test/Evaluate Prototype

	Apr	May	Jun	Jul	Aug	Sep	Oct	Nov	Dec	Plan	% C	Value
Test Plan Development	3									3	100	3
Unit Testing	2									2	100	2
Full Testing		4								4	100	4
Destructive Testing		4								4	50	2
Test Documentation		2								2	50	1
Monthly Plan	5	10	0	0	0	0	0	0	0	15	80	12

Table 2   Rollup of Percent Complete

The schedule variance in time (S) is shown along the time axis in Figure 4.

COMPARISON WITH USUAL PROJECT MANAGEMENT REPORTING METHODS

Usually, when project progress is reported, two types of information are presented: schedule data and cost data. Schedule data is typically shown in a Gantt (or similar type) chart, as shown in Figure 5 for the example project here. Cost data is typically reported as actual cost versus planned cost. The cost variance is often just reported at the total level as total actual cost incurred versus budget.

The problem with these usual methods is that they do not provide a clear quantitative picture of the true project status, and they do not provide a means for extrapolating project cost to complete or completion date. For our example project, when we look at the Gantt chart in Figure 5—which also shows the task percent complete as dark bar stripes inside the bars—and we see that we are not over budget—actual cost of $83,000 versus planned cost of $91,000—it is hard to say how much we are behind schedule, and it *appears we are not overspending.*

However, on this project, *we are well behind schedule and are overspending,* as the earned value analysis shows. The schedule variance is 0.67 months (behind schedule), and the cost variance is

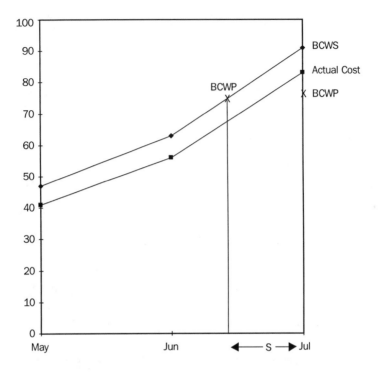

Figure 4 Earned Value Variances

$10,000 (overspent). The estimated time to complete is fifteen months instead of the twelve months planned, and the estimated cost to complete is $289,000 instead of $254,000. The exact calculation of these numbers is shown in Table 3 (discussed later).

CURRENT EARNED VALUE METHODS AND ASSOCIATED PROBLEMS

If earned value analysis is such a good measure of true project performance, then why is it not used more in industry? There appear to be several reasons for this. First, commercial awareness of earned value is minimal; corporate training courses rarely discuss earned value, and there is relatively little in commercial print on the subject. Second, the data acquisition required (for obtaining percent

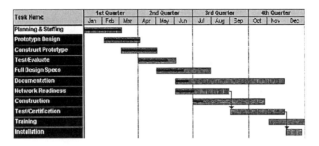

Figure 5 Gantt Chart Representing Project Schedule and Percent Complete

complete and actual cost numbers), if implemented in a by-the-book method, is too costly and time consuming. Third, earned value reporting has not been handled in an easily implemented manner. And last, there are significant employee and contractor resistance problems when trying to put earned value into practice.

OVERCOMING THE DATA ACQUISITION PROBLEMS

Providing for easy and effective data acquisition requires that the methodology used be relatively nonintrusive yet provides the necessary accuracy. *Nonintrusive* means that very little extra effort is required by project team members or managers to provide the input data for the analysis. The goal is to implement the necessary data acquisition as a byproduct of existing corporate reporting or payroll procedures when possible. Three key steps in the methodology are: 1) setting appropriate work packet size, 2) appropriate definition of percent complete, and, 3) appropriate basis for costing.

If work packets are too small, there will be excessive reporting and paperwork required by project members and managers. If work packets are too big, performance will not be measured frequently enough to allow corrective action. If project performance is to be measured monthly, the work packets should be smaller than a month, such as a week or two. It is best to tie the maximum size of work packets to the payroll data acquisition frequency, where employee labor is a significant cost item.

Percent complete estimates must be provided for each work packet on a regular reporting basis. For most work packets, taking the time to calculate the percent complete based on the amount of completed versus the amount of work remaining (or the number of *things* completed versus the number of *things* in the work packet) is too time consuming and an unnecessary burden on project members. If the work packet's size has been appropriately determined, then the packet estimates can be rough without losing much accuracy on the overall project performance evaluation. For example, a very easy percent complete scheme is:

- Have not begun work on packet   0%
- Working on packet   50%
- Finished packet   100%

If reporting is weekly for a one-year project and if the average work packet size is a week, then the maximum error (assuming current week's tasks estimated 50 percent in error, and all off in the same direction) would be (Average Packets Per Week * Average Cost Per Packet * 0.5)/(Total Cost), which reduces to (.5/52) or about 1 percent. Thus, if we had a project with a planned cost of $1,040,000 over a year with 520 work packets (average ten per week), the maximum error in analysis at each month end would still only be about 1 percent.

Earned value analysis requires a percent complete for each work packet, as shown in Table 2. This value requires knowledge of the planned cost and the percent complete; it does not require knowledge of the actual cost. Schedule variations can be calculated without any knowledge of actual costs. The earned value cost variance for the total project *only requires knowledge of the total project actual cost*, not individual work packet actual costs. A major problem in many organizations is that actual costs, even at the total project level, are not obtainable in a timely manner or properly segregated by project. In that case, it is necessary to set up a *feed-forward* cost-reporting system instead of a *feed-back* cost system, which usually comes off the company's general ledger. In this case, resource utilization is tracked as well as percent complete, and the predicted cost is the resources utilized times the estimated resource rate. For labor, the hours worked is tracked each reporting period, as well as the percent complete for each work packet. The hours worked are then multiplied by a *burdened* labor rate, either as an overall rate for the project or a rate for each skill level. This will introduce some errors, but compared, to overall project costs, these should be small. If a project consists mostly of labor, the process can be further simplified by representing earned value completely in hours instead of dollars.

OVERCOMING THE REPORTING PROBLEMS

Reporting earned value in many project-scheduling tools is usually not easy. This is for several reasons. First, getting actual costs into a project so that they can be used in the system's earned value mechanism usually means getting actual costs into each task and, in many systems, getting actual costs into the resources for each task. Second, setting up an automatic interface between your corporate systems (or departmental databases) and a project management system is not trivial, and usually does not use a standard format such as a spreadsheet. Third, using the earned value mechanism in these systems is not typically straightforward and simple.

As stated in the last section, actual costs or estimates thereof are only required for the entire project to find the cost variance and estimated cost at completion. A simple and straightforward way to do this is with a database product (i.e., Access, dBase, and so on) or spreadsheet, as shown in Table 3. This can be done manually, or interfaces to spreadsheet tools (i.e., Excel or Lotus) are relatively easy to set up.

When, and only when, there is a problem with a project do you need to *drill down* your earned-value cost-variance analysis to lower levels of the WBS; and only then for the WBS areas in which there appear to be a problem (management by exception). At that point, you need to look at a spreadsheet like Table 4, where the next-level-down WBS work plan has been augmented with actual costs (or estimates thereof).

OVERCOMING THE EMPLOYEE/CONTRACTOR RESISTANCE PROBLEMS

To be fully successful, any project-management performance-measurement system must be accepted by project team members and project managers. Thus, it is important that such performance systems be nonintrusive and directed primarily toward measuring projects, not individuals.

Project Earned Value Analysis—through July

	Jan	Feb	Mar	Apr	May	Jun	Jul	Aug	Sep	Oct	Nov	Dec	Plan	% C	Value
Planning and Staffing	3	2											5	100	5
Prototype Design		3	3										6	100	6
Construct Prototype			8	8									16	100	16
Test/Evaluate Prototype				5	10								15	80	12
Full Design Specs					5	6	3						14	50	7
Documentation						2	2	1	1	1	1		8	12	0.96
Site Preparation						8	3	3					14	36	5.04
Construction							20	50	50	20			140	15	21
Test/ Certification									10	6	4		20	0	0
Finishing											8	4	12	0	0
Maintenance Training												4	4	0	0
Monthly Plan	3	5	11	13	15	16	28	54	61	27	13	8	254		73
Cumulative	3	8	19	32	47	63	91	145	206	233	246	254			
Monthly Actual	4	4	10	11	12	15	27	0	0	0	0	0	83		
Cumulative Actual	4	8	18	29	41	56	83								

Schedule Variances

Budgeted Cost of Work Scheduled (BCWS)	91
Budgeted Cost of Work Performed (BCWP)	73
Schedule Variance (Dollars)	18
Schedule Variance (Months)	0.67
Schedule Efficiency Factor	0.80
Estimated Time to Complete (Months)	15

Cost Variances

Actual Cost of Work Performed (ACWP)	83
Budgeted Cost of Work Performed (BCWP)	73
Cost Variance (Dollars)	10
Cost Variance (Percent)	3.90
Cost Efficiency Factor	0.90
Estimated Cost at Completion	289

Table 3 Earned Value Analysis Spreadsheet

Test/Evaluate Prototype												
	Apr	May	Jun	Jul	Aug	Sep	Oct	Nov	Dec	Plan	% C	Value
Test Plan Development	3									3	100	3
Unit Testing	2									2	100	2
Full Testing		4								4	100	4
Destructive Testing		4								4	50	2
Test Documentation		2								2	50	1
Monthly Plan	5	10	0	0	0	0	0	0	0	15	80	12
Cumulative	5	15	15	15	15	15	15	15	15	15		
Monthly Actual	2	4	4	4								
Cumulative Actual	2	6	10	14								
Actual Cost of Work Performed						14						
Budgeted Cost of Work Performed						12						
Cost Variance (Dollars)						2						

Table 4   Earned Value *Drill Down*

Since earned value analysis provides a level of insight deep into the project workings, it is likely to be viewed by some as a means of employee (and/or contractor) evaluation instead of project performance evaluation. The best way to address this issue is to adopt earned value methodology along with some form of total quality management (TQM); if TQM (or a similar effort) is already in place, seal earned value within that other envelope. Management must focus on the use of earned value for extrapolation of project cost to complete, estimation of actual completion date, knowledge of project trouble areas (so resources/plans can be adjusted), and refinement of work-packet estimation methods, and not the use of earned value for individual evaluations.

INTEGRATION WITH EXECUTIVE INFORMATION SYSTEMS

Earned value methods have another advantage over current reporting techniques (Gantt charts and cost versus budget). Since earned values are quantitative numbers expressed in dollars (for both cost and schedule deviations), these numbers can be rolled up along an OBS—for example, to give a picture of how all projects are performing in an

Project	BCWS	BCWP	Time Var ($)	Var +	ACWP	Cost Var ($)	Var +	Plan	EAC
Project 1	91	73	18	18	83	10	10	254	289
Project 2	130	135	-5	0	125	-10	0	302	302
Project 3	65	60	5	5	75	15	15	127	159
Project 4	25	23	2	2	27	4	4	48	56
Project 5	84	82	2	2	81	-1	0	180	180
Project 6	53	47	6	6	48	1	1	110	112
Project 7	102	103	-1	0	110	7	7	190	203
Project 8	35	37	-2	0	40	3	3	78	84
	585	**560**			**589**				**1385**

Total Schedule Variance	33	Total Cost Variance	40
Relative Schedule Variance	5.64%	Relative Cost Variance	6.84%
Schedule Variance (Months)	0.68	Cost at Completions	1385

Table 5 Reporting Multiple Projects

organization. Since underspent projects do not necessarily help over-spent projects (in either time or dollars), often the negative variations are set to zero, and estimate at completion is unchanged. This is illustrated in Table 5. If spreadsheet models are used for earned value, such as in Table 5, then these are easily interfaced with most executive information systems.

SUMMARY

Earned value analysis is a very powerful project management tool. If an organization can effectively integrate this tool into its procurement, timekeeping, and executive information systems, then it is probably the single best method for measuring and reporting true project performance and estimating time and cost to complete. This article has presented some methodology that can yield an effective and relatively easy integration of these systems including appropriate work packet sizing, simple yet accurate estimation of work packet percent complete, feed-forward actual cost acquisition, simple spreadsheet (or database) reporting methods, and use of a quality management envelope.

References

Abba, Wayne. (n.d.). Earned Value Management Rediscovered. [Online]. Available: http://www.acq.osd.mil/pm/newpolicy/misc/abba_art.html

Christensen, David S., J. McKinney, and R. Antooni. 1995. A Review of Estimate at Completion Research. *Journal of Cost Analysis* (Spring).

Fleming, Quentin, and Joel Koppelman. 1994. The Essence of Evolution of Earned Value. *Cost Engineering* 36.11: 21–27.

———. 1996. *Earned ValueProject Management.* Upper Darby, PA: Project Management Institute.

Hewitt, Leland, and Michael O'Connor. 1993. Applying Earned Value to Government In-House Activities. *Army Research, Development & Acquisition Bulletin* (Jan.–Feb.): 8–10.

Horan, Ron, and Don McNichols. 1990. Project Management for Large Systems. *Business Communications Review* 20 (Sept.): 15–24.

When the DIPP* Dips: A P&L Index for Project Decisions

Stephen A. Devaux, Analytic Project Management, Bedford, Massachusetts

Project Management Journal 22.3 (Sept. 1992)

> *DIPP—DeVaux' Index of Project Performance—is defined in the text of this article.

FEW MANAGEMENT DECISIONS are more difficult than to determine whether to keep funding a project or to abandon it. And few decisions are more crucial to corporate health; a sick project can be a sinkhole into which enormous amounts of money disappear with little hope of return.

Methodologies are appearing to help identify and evaluate troubled projects. Suresh K. Tadisina (1986) performed statistical discriminant analysis on data for about 220 R&D projects. By categorizing them as successes or failures, he isolated twenty-three major factors that seemed to be suitable predictors. With the possible caveat of tautologous reasoning (abandoned projects were automatically listed as failures, without examination of whether or not the decision was correct), this technique may be useful for indepth analysis once a potential problem has been identified.

But the Tadisina system is complex, and its data are not easily accessible. It requires many subjective judgments (complexity of the project, implications for users), and is generally unsuitable as a monitoring index. Similarly, Shafer and Mantel (1989) recommend a weighted model to support decisions. Again, their model is complex, and it suggests that a decrease in a project's *score* from one period to the next might justify its termination. However, in reality, a project's historical data should be part of the decision *only* insofar as it is used to establish reliability about current data and forecasts. The decision to go on or stop should always be based on current status and forecasts, not history.

Meredith (1988) proposes an ongoing "audit" of the project, based on several criteria. But, these criteria also suffer from subjectivity (e.g., Is commitment dissipating? Is there organizational inertia?) and complexity. Profit and loss, which can be quantified and should be at the heart of the decision, is only one of many factors.

These articles emphasize the need for some sort of index of project profitability. Tadisina says, "To be useful, the monitoring mechanism should be inexpensive and easy to implement and operate." None of the methodologies seem to respond fully to that need. What follows is a system with an easily comprehended index, which can be computed quickly.

THE METHODOLOGY

Earned value calculations allow management to measure the amount of work that has been performed, the *bang* they've been getting for their *buck*, and to estimate future costs. These methodologies are readily available, but their implications for a *go/no-go* decision are rarely quantified.

There is no dispute that the go/no-go decision must always involve considerations beyond dollars. Factors such as the media fallout of abandoning a well-publicized project, legal implications, losing a market niche, the human costs in layoffs, morale damage, and internal cynicism need to be analyzed. These and other issues may often outweigh the purely financial evaluation. However, the economic considerations should be isolated from the other factors and kept in focus at the center of the discussion. All other data should be treated as modifiers, brightening or darkening the picture that counting the dollars has painted. In that way, management will be in a position to say, "Yes, we're going to take a loss of $X on this project. But that seems a small price to pay for ... "

In trying to establish precisely where to start the search for meaningful data, it is important to consider the project life cycle. Figures 1, 2, and 3 show a typical product development project at

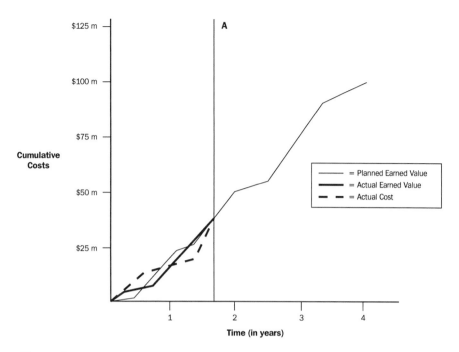

Figure 1

different points in the life cycle. This type of project serves as a suitable paradigm because the financial numbers involved in product development (whether in construction, software development, pharmaceuticals, engineering, or publishing) are often a little clearer than in other types of projects.

For our example, we will consider a hypothetical four-year, $100 million project to develop, manufacture, and market a product expected to generate $150 million in sales. For simplicity's sake, we will assume that all dollars are *real* dollars (zero inflation during the life of the project) and that the sales revenue will be received as soon as the product is delivered.

We will now analyze three *real-world* problems. You are the CEO who must make the decisions. For purposes of this exercise, you should consider *only* the economics of the situation.

1. In Figure 1, at time A, eighteen months after start, our project is on schedule and on budget. We have achieved one quarter of the project's total earned value with actual costs of $25 million. However,

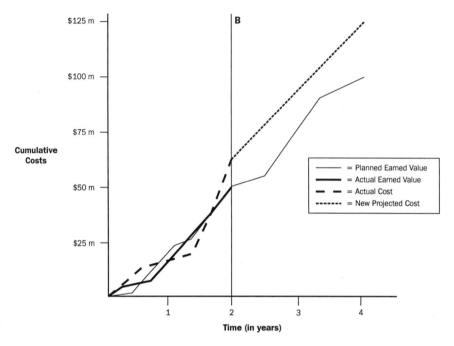

Figure 2

new market research shows that a competitor will beat us to market by a full year with a similar product. This is expected to cut our total market share and our contribution margin to $70 million. Should you approve further expenditure on this project or abandon it?

2. In Figure 2, at time B, after two years, the latest market study shows projected sales holding steady and the contribution margin at $70 million. However, our project has run into problems. Instead of being half finished, we have completed only 40 percent of the work. We have already spent $60 million, and we now estimate that it will cost another $65 million to complete it. Go? Or no go?

3. In Figure 3, the project has reached time C. It has been one problem after another. We have already spent $100 million. Our estimate-to-complete stands at an additional $30 million. Further delays have lowered our market share to the point where we can expect to make only one-third of our original contribution margin of $150 million. Fish? Or cut bait?

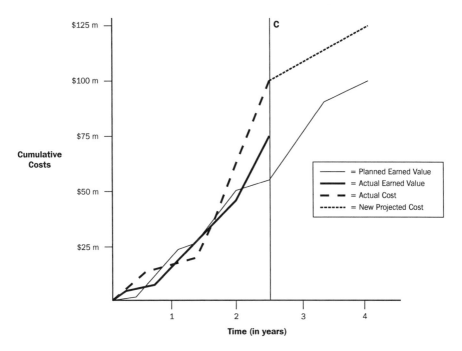

Figure 3

These decisions are all painful ones. In every case, the company is going to lose money and, in situations 2 and 3, a great deal of money. In such dilemmas, there are two very human temptations: to let the inertia of the project dictate a *nondecision* decision, thus allowing it to finish; or, with a macho decisiveness, to shut one's eyes to the numbers and one's ears to the screams while amputating the offending project.

Yet, this decision is precisely the kind that can save a company millions. It should be analyzed and reasoned with clearest logic, and hard numbers should be relied upon wherever possible.

Situation 1. In situation one, we have a project that has been proceeding smoothly, with neither schedule nor cost variance. Yet suddenly, due to an unforeseen occurrence in the marketplace, our anticipated contribution margin from the finished product has fallen by $80 million. Obviously, there is no longer much chance of producing the cool $50 million in contribution margin for which we had hoped. But, should we abandon the project?

	Millions of Dollars
Actual cost-to-date	25
Estimate-to-complete	75
Total cost at completion	100
Total project contribution margin	70
Total contribution if completed (100 - 70)	30
Total contribution losses if halted	25
Relevant contribution if halted	- 5
DIPP = .933	

Table 1 Economic Analysis of Situation 1

First, we must divest ourselves of all consideration of what went before. Yes, we have already invested $25 million. And yes, this project is doomed to lose money. But those are not the issues. Sunk costs are not relevant costs. In this and all other such cases, the discussion must be pared down to this question: From this moment on, can we save the company more money by proceeding or by halting? When examined in this light, we discover the numbers in Table 1.

Halting the project will therefore save the company $5 million. Unless an alternative can be found, which will alter the current outlook (shorten the project duration and beat the competitor to market, for instance), the project should probably be abandoned.

An important lesson may be drawn from this example. The fact that a project is proceeding smoothly is not necessarily an indication that it should be completed. The implication of this is that, in a product development project, the project manager needs to keep one eye on the marketplace at all times. An appropriate tool for doing this will be suggested later.

Situation 2. In the second situation, the project has fallen behind schedule and is also over budget. You might assume that this would seal its fate all the more. Yet, we cannot be sure without again examining the numbers (see Table 2).

In this case, if the project is halted, it will cost the company $5 million more than to complete it, according to the present plan. The reason for the change is that the project's estimate-to-complete has

	Millions of Dollars
Actual cost-to-date	60
Estimate-to-complete	65
Total cost at completion	125
Total project contribution margin	70
Total contribution if completed (125 - 70)	55
Total contribution losses if halted	60
Relevant contribution if halted	+ 5
DIPP = 1.077	

Table 2   Economic Analysis of Situation 2

been reduced as work has gone on. With much of the course already run, it probably makes economic sense to complete the product.

Situation 3. In the third situation, we can expect to make only $50 million, down $100 million from our original lofty goal. Surely, we should cut this one loose! But let us again scrutinize the numbers (see Table 3).

This time, if the project is halted, it will cost the company $20 million more than to complete it according to the present plan. Obviously, as the project nears completion, the expected revenues needed to justify its completion shrink to a tiny fraction of the original projections. In this case, a bare $30 million, or 20 percent of the original estimate, would have been the fulcrum.

A clear pattern has emerged: In every case, the margin on which the decision rests is the difference between the total projected sales and the estimate-to-complete. This not only emphasizes that sunk costs are not meaningful when making the go/no-go decision on a project; but it also provides us with an important and easily generated index:

Devaux's Index of Project Performance (DIPP) =

$$DIPP = \frac{\text{Total Project Contribution Margin (TPCM)}}{\text{Estimate-to-Complete (ETC)}}$$

	Millions of Dollars
Actual cost-to-date	100
Estimate-to-complete	30
Total cost at completion	130
Total project contribution margin	50
Total contribution if completed (130 - 50)	80
Total contribution losses if halted	100
Relevant contribution if halted	+ 20
DIPP = 1.667	

Table 3 Economic Analysis of Situation 3

The DIPP should be used as a threshold index for all product development projects. Whenever the DIPP dips below 1.0 (in other words, total projected sales become equal to or less than estimate-to-complete), it will almost certainly cost more to complete the project than to halt it. But the simple fact that the DIPP is above 1.0 does not necessarily mean that the project is still profitable; other considerations that bear on profitability should be examined and, wherever possible, quantified. Some of these are listed below.

Refinement 1: Opportunity Cost

If resources were unlimited, this would never be a factor. However, since most companies are constrained by available labor, equipment, materials, and/or finances, opportunity cost is a commonly invoked reason for abandoning a project.

Yet, all too often this is merely a rationalization. Opportunity cost should only be factored into the equation if there really is no other way of obtaining a resource. If the resource can be duplicated but only at great expense, then the expense incurred should be included in the equation as an opportunity cost. But just because the same resource can be used on another project does not justify canceling the original project if in so doing an unnecessary loss is incurred. If it is possible to duplicate the resource, then both projects should be completed.

The inclusion of opportunity cost amends the DIPP as follows:

$$DIPP = \frac{TPCM - OC}{ETC} = 1.0$$

In situation 2, if the opportunity cost of completing the project is estimated at \$5 million, this would lower the DIPP to exactly 1.0.

$$DIPP = \frac{\$70\ mil - \$5\ mil}{\$65\ mil}$$

Refinement 2: Cannibalization Worth

As work is performed on one project (e.g., equipment purchases, landscaping, skill training, acquiring process patents), it frequently has potential value for other projects. The value of the work that can be transferred can affect the DIPP. But (and this is crucial!) *only* insofar as the transfer destroys the value of the work for the original project. Otherwise, the transfer has no implications for the validity of pursuing the original project.

For instance, let us suppose that we build an access road in preparation for constructing a shopping mall. Then, it turns out that an apartment complex would be even more profitable. If there is room on the site for one or the other but not both, then the value of the road may be transferred to the apartment project. This would increase the return necessary to justify completing the mall. However, if the site is large enough to contain both structures, the road's value should not be cannibalized: the mall project should be considered as separate from the apartment project.

This *moveable* value is like opportunity cost, except that it relates to work already completed rather than resources for work to be done in the future. This value is referred to as the *cannibalization worth* (CW) of the project. It has the effect of increasing the level of total projected sales necessary to justify completing the project. It can be included in the DIPP equation as follows:

$$DIPP = \frac{TPCM - OC - CW}{ETC}$$

In situation 2, a cannibalization worth of \$2 million would be sufficient to justify stopping the project (see Table 4).

	Millions of Dollars
Estimate-to-complete	65
Total project contribution margin	70
Opportunity cost	5
Cannibalization worth	2

$$DIPP = \frac{\$70\ mil - \$5\ mil - \$2\ mil}{\$65\ mil} = \frac{63}{65} = .97$$

Table 4 Effect for Opportunity Cost and Cannibalization

Refinement 3: Project Termination Cost

Frequently, there is cost associated with abandoning a project: Materials must be stored, equipment sold, and unemployment insurance paid. All these contribute to the argument for continuing the project. As a result, their costs should be subtracted from the estimate-to-complete in the DIPP formula:

$$DIPP = \frac{TPCM - OC - CW}{ETC - PTC}$$

In situation 3, a PTC of $3 million would send the DIPP for our project back above 1.0 (see Table 5).

Refinement 4: Computing Total Project Revenue

For simplicity's sake, all of the situations we have examined have treated sales revenue as though it were a lump sum to be received upon completion of the project. But, normally, the product will be bringing in revenue over several years. Even without allowing for inflation, the value of a dollar received three years hence is not the same as one received today. This is sometimes referred to as the *time value of money*.

Future revenues may be discounted by using net present value analysis. According to this formula, the amount of money received for a product each year after delivery to market is divided by $(1 + i)$ to the power n, where i is projected interest rate on the money and

	Millions of Dollars
Estimate-to-complete	65
Total project contribution margin	70
Opportunity cost	5
Cannibalization worth	2
Project termination cost	3

$$DIPP = \frac{\$70\ mil - \$5\ mil - \$2\ mil}{\$65\ mil - \$3\ mil} = \frac{63}{62} = 1.02$$

Table 5   Effect of Opportunity Cost and Project Termination Cost

n is the number of years after delivery. According to this formula, the TPCM would be derived as shown:

$$TPCM_{NPV} = TPCM\ Now + \frac{(TPCM\ y_1)}{(1+i)^1} + \frac{(TPCM\ y_2)}{(1+i)^2} + \ldots + \frac{(TPR\ y_n)}{(1+i)^n}$$

Thus, if we estimate an annual interest rate of 10 percent, we can break down the TPCM for situation two as shown in Table 6.

CONCLUSION

What are the implications of all this?

First, the circumstances surrounding the reexamination of a troubled project are often chaotic. Emotions can run high, and attention is often focused on issues that are irrelevant. ("We've already spent *eleventeen* million dollars developing this widget. Let's not waste it." Or alternatively: "Let's not throw good money after bad!" The DIPP formula helps reduce some of these issues to quantifiable data.

Second, the DIPP isolates the financial data from other considerations. While many of the efforts of previous authors have been to provide a single index that would take all factors into account, I suggest that such an approach might be a mistake. It is important to be able to focus on just the economics of the decision.

Third, the link between product development and the marketplace is drawn all the more tightly. The development project cannot

	Millions of Dollars
$TPCM_{NPV}$ Now $= 5.0/1.0$	5.0
$TPCM_{NPV}$ Yr 1 $= 25/1.1 =$	22.7
$TPCM_{NPV}$ Yr 2 $= 25/1.21 =$	12.4
$TPCM_{NPV}$ Yr 3 $= 10/1.33 =$	7.5
$TPCM_{NPV}$ Yr 4 $= 10/1.46 =$	6.8
$TPCM_{NPV}$ Yr 5 $= 5/1.61 =$	3.1
	57.5

Now the total TPR for use in the DIPP equation would be:

$$TPCM = 5.0 + 22.7 + 12.4 + 7.5 + 6.8 + 3.1 = \$57.5 \; mil$$

$$DIPP = \frac{\$57.5 \; mil - \$5 \; mil - \$2 \; mil}{\$65 \; mil - \$3 \; mil}$$

$$= \frac{\$50.2}{62} = .81$$

Table 6   Effect of Net Present Value on Cash Flow

be separated from the sales forecast. This suggests that the project manager on such projects must also be the *product* manager, keeping one eye on market forecasts at all time. This may allow the product manager to make duration and/or budget changes in the project on the basis of market conditions. For example, a project's DIPP might be below 1.0 when computed on the basis of the current operating plan, but a change in that plan might increase the DIPP. Increases or cuts in scope, budget, or project duration can all affect the total project revenue, the estimate-to-complete, or both.

Perhaps most important, the DIPP should be used as an *early-warning* indicator. Reports to senior management should include this index, at least in its simplest form, (i.e., DIPP = TPCM/ETC). The DIPP can then be used to establish an escalation threshold, much as schedule variance (SV) and cost variance (CV) are often used. A suggestion would be that anytime the DIPP falls below 1.0 + .2n (where n = the remaining duration in years or parts of years), senior management be alerted, the refined DIPP computed, and the project plan scrutinized. In other words, if a project is in its final year, its simple DIPP would need to be greater than 1.2; in its last two years, greater than 1.4; and so on. In this way, corrective actions that might forestall the eventual cancellation of the project could be taken.

Acknowledgment

The author would like to express sincere thanks to Wayne Halverson and Walter Frank for their valuable insights and assistance.

References

Meredith, J. R. 1988. Project Monitoring for Early Termination. *Project Management Journal* 19.5: 31–38.

Shafer, S. M., and S. J. Mantel. 1989. A Decision Support System for the Project Termination Decision: A Spreadsheet Approach. *Project Management Journal* 20.2: 23–28.

Staw, B. M., and J. Ross. 1988. Knowing When to Pull the Plug. *Harvard Business Review* (Mar.–Apr.): 68–74.

Tadisina, S. K. 1986. Support Systems for the Termination Decision in R&D Management. *Project Management Journal* 17.5: 97–104.

Planning for Crises in Project Management

Larry A. Mallak, Department of Industrial and Manufacturing Engineering, Western Michigan University
Harold A. Kurstedt, Jr, Virginia Polytechnic Institute and State University
Gerold A. Patzak, Technical University of Vienna

Project Management Journal 28.2 (June 1997)

P ROJECT MANAGERS CANNOT always foresee every contingency when planning and managing their projects. Many spurious events affecting project milestones and resource allocations can surface once the project is under way. Experienced project managers find crises, miscommunications, mistakes, oversights, and disasters must be managed as part of successful project management. They need effective tools to anticipate and prepare for these crises. These are tools that project managers may not use every day, yet they need them in emergencies. The ideas and information in this article will help project managers identify the appropriate crisis-planning tools and how to use them. The project manager's experience, training, and skills should allow for understanding and use of these emergency management tools to support quicker and better decision-making. In a crisis, the worst decision is no decision, and the second worst decision is a late one (Sawle 1991). Managing crises better means mitigating and preparing for crises, so we can reduce their occurrences and manage the consequences better if crises do occur. Based on the authors' experiences in emergency management for the public and private sectors and several experiences shared in the literature, we recommend ways of planning for crises in projects.

We offer a brief list of emergency-management planning tools and skills for project managers: risk analyses, contingency plans, logic charts, and tabletop exercises. These tools have different uses in different types of crises, whether they are natural, chemical/technological, or security types of crises. They also require different kinds of support—police, fire, medical, rescue, and so on.

Crises are analyzed from the project management perspective, identifying the similarities and differences between crises in project management and crises in general. We discuss crisis-planning strategies and tools by looking at the tools used for emergency management and investigating how we can modify them, or design new tools for crisis management in projects.

FRAMING THE CRISIS

Many crises become projects once the deleterious effects are gone. A commercial airline crash, such as TWA 800 in summer 1996, where all passengers and crew died, is managed as a project once the threat of explosion and other immediate dangers diminish. However, we're concerned with crises occurring within an existing project, rather than a crisis or emergency that becomes a project.

In many of emergency management's phases and types, the primary skills required are project management skills with which we're already familiar. When we 're in an emergency situation, and we are in the mitigation, preparedness, or recovery phase in a chronic, long-term emergency, we can readily apply our project management skills. The focus of this article is the use of emergency management tools to aid in anticipating and planning for crises in projects. Project managers need additional tools to respond to acute emergencies. (Here is where emergency management tools become paramount.)

The scope of application for emergency management tools will vary, based on the size of the project. The tools can be quite elaborate, such as volumes for a risk analysis or reserved space for an emergency operations center (EOC) with many dedicated phone lines. The tools can also be quite simple, such as a one- to two-page listing of risks in priority order, or a designated office or conference room (to function as a mini-EOC) with the ability to bring in portable phones. All of the tools should be used, even if only in simple form. In a small project, using one hour of a staff meeting to assign roles in the event of a crisis may suffice for more elaborate means in a larger project. The elaborateness of tools should be balanced with the cost and time required for preparation.

Typical project management requires attention to issues of cost, schedule, and quality. As the customer demands for quality increase, either the cost or the schedule must yield to balance these new demands. But, at what point do increased demands reach a crisis point? Increased demands may lead to a perplexity. A perplexity is "an event with an unknown start and an unknown end." An example of a perplexity is an earthquake centered on the New Madrid (Mo.) fault line—we do not know when the earthquake will occur, for how long, nor what the extent of damage will be. In fact, the earthquake may not occur in our lifetime. The opposite of a perplexity is a process, an event with a known start and a known end, and the cycle is constantly repeated (as in a manufacturing process). The concept of perplexity helps to understand the amount and level of uncertainty faced in emergency planning for projects.

In this article, a crisis could be externally generated, as in an earthquake, deregulation, loss of key executives through accidental death (airplane or automobile crash), or internally generated, as in a plant explosion or a strike. We use Lagadec's (1993) definition of a crisis as being an incident that upsets normal conditions, creating a disturbance that cannot be brought back to normal by using existing or specialized emergency functions. A crisis, according to Lagadec, can occur when the incident passes a certain level, or when the system is unstable or was close to the breaking point before the incident took place. Consequently, crises considered in this paper disrupt project activities to the point when new (and typically unanticipated) decisions must be made to continue the project.

Projects have characteristics that make the design and preparation of elaborate tools difficult. First, many projects lack the permanence of a mine, large plant, or government installation. Second, emergencies in smaller projects tend to be more constrained to the site, while larger projects must deal with emergencies of greater scope and impact, such as chemical and radiological releases. Third, in a plant, a large number of people are affected by an emergency—especially the public, as opposed to the workers. When the public or a large number of workers are involved, the organization's confidence in safe operations has a heavy influence, and this begets elaborateness. A simple tool can afford us most of the protection we need (for example, 70 percent of maximum), while a more elaborate tool will buy us more confidence and protection (perhaps up to 99 percent of maximum). The more elaborate tool is worth the investment when confidence is at stake.

TOOLS TO HELP PROJECT MANAGERS PLAN FOR CRISES

We've chosen four types of tools used primarily in emergency management to help project managers better plan for crises. We will describe and show how to apply risk analyses, contingency plans, logic charts, and tabletop exercises.

Risk Analysis. An essential crisis-planning tool is risk analysis. Risk analysis helps us discover what can go wrong, what is most probable, and what has the greatest impact. The combination of an event's probability of occurrence and severity of consequences (e.g., catastrophic failure) determines priorities. Incident analysis can also help us understand the lessons learned in an actual crisis, and develop plans to mitigate the effects of similar incidents in the future.

The 1996 Olympic Games in Atlanta presented many potential disruptions to area businesses (Bradford 1996). Comprehensive contingency plans were needed to increase the potential for business continuity. Atlanta-based BellSouth Business Systems Director of Business Continuity Services John Copenhaver stated, "If you plan for a medium-case scenario and a worst-case scenario happens, it's like having no plans at all." BellSouth's plan attempted to minimize disruptions during the Olympics through special arrangements for deliveries, telecommuting, and increased modem pools so employees could work from home. BellSouth conducted a vulnerability assessment and then put systems into place to avoid interruptions to service or minimize the impact of interruptions.

Another Bell company, BellSouth Advertising and Publishing Co. (BAPCO), saw the need to develop a plan to deal with the human side of crises (traumatic stress), because these could disable a firm just as well as interruption of normal business operations—e.g., phone, equipment, facilities (Kruse 1993). BAPCO brought in a consultant team to deliver a one-day crisis-management training session. The training was given to members of a human-resources crisis team and other members of management who wanted to participate. Through counseling, housing, BellMart, rental cars, and other support mechanisms, BAPCO weathered Hurricane Andrew much better than most South Florida organizations. BellMart was a stocked warehouse of essentials that BAPCO employees (and even their non-BAPCO neighbors) were invited to visit and take whatever they needed. Eighty-five percent of BAPCO employees were affected by the hurricane although none were killed. The company pointed to several initiatives that were taken to reduce traumatic stress so that people could return to work sooner and with fewer worries. These initiatives included a rapid deployment system to immediately attend to their employees' needs, determining those needs in advance, heading off traumatic stress with constant information—daily bulletins issued; people sought by phone, foot, car, and so on; bringing in BAPCO volunteers from other areas; making cash available immediately; and giving employees time off from work to get their personal lives together.

Sometimes nature surprises us, and sometimes nature tests us. The Virginia Department of Transportation (VDOT) had an opportunity to test its emergency preparedness in a potential disaster that never materialized (Slack 1996). Hurricane Bertha threatened to slam into Virginia as a full-force hurricane, but weakened into a tropical gale with heavy winds and rain—not the widespread destruction of a hurricane. Bertha served as a drill for VDOT's Emergency Operations Center, which used a new computer system designed to keep various safety agencies up to date with the latest information during a crisis. One of the problems VDOT faced during many natural disasters was conflicting information among VDOT, state police, local police, and other state agencies involved in emergency response. All parties now have the same information via a real-time connection, and are able to work together, rather than each agency gathering its own information.

The availability of accurate, real-time information is not enough to mitigate crises in project management. Good implementation of risk analysis helps to plan and properly prepare for crises in projects, and take steps to reduce the occurrences of crises. Engineering analyses support this process of risk analysis and make up the quantitative portion of mitigation. Cause-and-effect analyses make up the qualitative portion of mitigation, and help us assess the systematic effects both forward and backward.

In emergency management, we use risk analysis to discover the risks beforehand. The use of risk analysis in this article should be differentiated from a probabilistic risk analysis. Establishing the consequences of accidents or incidents by deterministic or risk analysis provides effective tools in emergency management. In project management, we concentrate on planning and sequencing activities to maximize our efficiencies and effectively schedule resources.

Illinois Power (IP) has a risk analysis process, called the Risk Register, which was developed and implemented in 1988 and serves as a comprehensive risk-assessment system. "The Risk Register is a formal process that identifies, quantifies, and categorizes the risks facing Illinois Power, develops cost-effective methods to control them, and positions the company to achieve its stated goals" (Leonard 1995). The system continually assesses new risks, generates information for decision-making, and supports employees at all levels.

Illinois Power's Risk-Register process has five phases: risk analysis, mitigation development, mitigation selection, implementation, and monitoring. In conjunction with the Risk Register, IP has a corporate disaster recovery plan, designed to "obtain information on levels of damage, resource availability, and the status of restoration activities; provide timely and accurate information to the media, government officials, regulatory authorities, employees, and the general public; give guidance on restoration activities; coordinate acquisition and allocation of resources and coordinate operations with city, county, state and federal emergency-service operations" (Leonard 1995).

For each identified risk, IP chooses a post-loss goal; in other words, the minimum acceptable capabilities following an event. The post-loss goal sets the target for what the crisis-management tool should help IP achieve, and helps reduce uncertainty during and after an event.

Contingency Plans. Once the risk analysis is performed, project managers must translate those risks into contingency plans. Project managers need to sit down, and ask, "What can go wrong with my project?" Once identified, the project manager has a list of risks associated with a particular project—the output of a risk analysis. Then, they should ask, "Which of these risks is most likely to happen?" and "Which of these will have the greatest impact?" "On what or whom?" This last question implies the vulnerability of the organization to the identified risks. Project managers should develop plans that use the data from a risk analysis to prepare them and their organizations for the broadest range of emergencies.

Appointing a person to be in charge of crisis planning puts responsibility and resources together, thereby reducing the need to overload already busy executives with planning for a low-probability event. Nestle U.S.A. Inc.'s headquarters are in Glendale, California, a suburb of Los Angeles. To support its contingency-planning efforts, Nestle has appointed a director of business-interruption planning (Ceniceros 1995). As part of its contingency plan, Nestle has a contract with the Stouffer Renaissance Esmeralda, a resort hotel in the desert near Palm Springs, stipulating that the hotel has three days to empty its ballroom if Nestle needs the space to resume business. The hotel was selected because it is already set to provide comfort, food, and beverages, and that relieves the demands on Nestle managers and counselors—so they can get back into serving their customers more rapidly and effectively. "Concern for personnel in planning for business resumption is just as important as facilities or data recovery" (Ceniceros 1995). Nestle has contracts with work-area-recovery vendors that have seventy-two hours to deliver office materials to the hotel. The hotel is accessible from an airport in Palm Springs, which expands access from Phoenix, should supplies need to come from elsewhere.

Nestle's contingency plan was tested with good results. "With the help of two furniture installation specialists and some hotel staff, the ballroom can quickly convert into 300 workstations complete with copy machines, computers, telecommunication cables, double-circuited power distribution panels, and everything else workers usually take for granted, such as sound barriers so business can be conducted with minimal distractions. ... At our last exercise, we pulled together 100 workstations in 20 clock hours" (Ceniceros 1995).

Risk analyses support planning by helping project managers choose the most probable and most severe events combined with a vulnerability assessment to see who or what is vulnerable, and what will be affected. Therefore, when the crisis occurs, the project manager has thought about the crisis and what can be affected. Plans incorporating this thinking help the project manager prepare for the crisis, and do what is necessary to fix it. If a manager is responsible for a project, he should require that someone conduct a risk analysis. The risk analysis improves early recognition of warning signs; the vulnerability assessment helps identify whom to notify and how to start support early.

Logic Charts. Logic charts employ project-flow logic to show the project flow with all dependencies in an extremely flexible, time-scale-independent diagram. Logic charts represent a form of expert system, because they embody the decision-making knowledge of the expert in a system that can be followed procedurally. Project-flow logic is the basis for any personal computer-assisted project management tool. Project managers are skilled at charting. But, in times of crisis, different types of charts are needed.

When a crisis occurs, people need procedures to follow. Logic charts form the basis for writing these procedures. In project management, the most commonly used charts are Gantt charts, for looking at activities against time, and networks, for looking at precedence. Emergency logic charts depend heavily on logic because of branching due to chained contingencies (e.g., "if event A and event B happened, then event C is likely").

Logic charts provide an overview of principal emergency-response events and recovery operations. The charts also depict decisions, notifications, support requests, and public information actions. Use of properly prepared charts take the affected site personnel through event discovery, event assessment, identification of emergency classification level, and to the activation of on-site response actions.

Logic charts force project managers to think through necessary critical decisions in a crisis. Project managers will not have time to go through the logic chart when the actual emergency occurs. The project manager must learn from the preparation and thinking required to construct a logic chart and feed it into or reinforce it through a tabletop exercise. When the crisis occurs, the project manager is not thinking as clearly as usual, and the more that is done before the crisis occurs, the better actions the project manager can take.

The Oak Ridge Office of the United States Department of Energy used logic charts in its emergency response and recovery operations. Its logic charts offered specific steps to take based on the type of event. The first step was event discovery, where provisions for an initial response were depicted. This resulted in an event assessment, leading to an initial emergency classification. Four levels of emergency classification followed, each evoking a particular response: a hazardous materials *usual event* (nonradiological), a hazardous materials *alert*, a *site emergency*, and a *general emergency*. A logic chart corresponding to the event discovery and initial response logic is shown in Figure 1.

Tabletop Exercises. Tabletops and other exercises use the information from the risk analysis in the mitigation phase to simulate the decision-making and action-taking occurring in an actual crisis. A tabletop exercise involves assembling the people who will be responding to a crisis and acting out possible scenarios in advance,

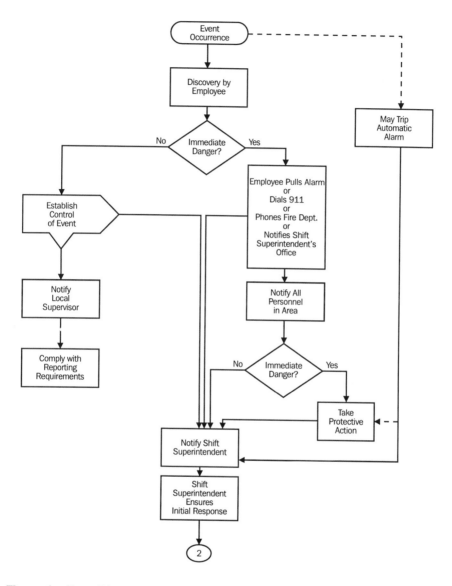

Figure 1 Event Discovery and Initial Response Logic Chart

usually in a conference room or similar space. There, without the pressure of time or the actual crisis, people have the freedom to discuss alternatives and decide on the best courses of action in a given situation. Tabletops also provide an opportunity to rehearse necessary steps in a potential crisis. These same techniques can help project managers prepare for possible crises in their own projects.

The events or crises occurring to project managers will not be the things being tracked. What we do not track is what will go wrong. The need for tracking illustrates the use of a structured management process to catch the small problems through a systematic, frequent, and thorough review of relevant indicators (Kurstedt, Mallak and Pacifici 1992).

Gershanov (1995) offers a five-stage process for holding tabletop exercises. Stage one identifies significant policy issues surrounding disasters in the organization. This identification may be conducted using an assessment tool, reviewing documents on responses to previous disasters, researching competitors' experiences, and reviewing debriefings of past exercises. Stage two examines these issues and isolates appropriate discussion questions. These discussion questions must be appropriate to the participant's level of responsibility in the organization. Discussion questions should address policy-level rather than operations-level concerns. Stage three is the tabletop exercise itself. According to Gershanov, one realistic scenario that encompasses the essential issues and problems should drive the exercise. A written version of the scenario should be available for the participants to refer to during the exercise. An outside facilitator with experience in emergency preparedness planning should run the exercise. Stage four is the debriefing of the exercise, providing a basis for further action and bringing a sense of closure to the exercise. Stage five, follow-up planning, concerns how the outcomes of the debriefing will be handled and getting commitment to developing plans based on the tabletop exercise.

Tabletop exercises were used in planning for security for the 1996 Democratic National Convention (DNC) in Chicago (O'Connor 1996). The Federal Emergency Management Agency facilitated tabletop exercises with members of the Chicago Police Department, the FBI, and the Secret Service to examine various scenarios and plan what would be done. Chicago Police also observed training and security practices for the 1996 Atlanta Olympic Games for lessons they could bring back to the DNC in Chicago.

Tabletop exercises are generally used in the beginning of crisis planning and focus on managerial information flows—who we talk to, what we do, who needs what information, and so forth. Issues surface in tabletops. Tabletops are a training device used to elicit understanding by carefully guiding the participants through a simulated emergency requiring a response. Although tabletop exercises are typically less expensive to conduct than drills or field exercises, they cannot substitute for the simulation of actual emergency events available through drills and field exercises.

Tabletop exercises should be conducted every quarter to keep emergency plans, procedures, and necessary thinking fresh in project managers' minds. Thinking through the decisions beforehand in an evaluative session such as a tabletop pays off when a real crisis occurs.

Tabletop exercises force managers to think through the decisions made during a crisis in advance, thereby reducing the need for decision-making during the crisis and reducing the time needed to make those decisions. "A tabletop is accomplished in controlled phases to allow discrete, individual answers, which focuses group attention on each point and thereby promotes a common understanding of roles and responsibilities and the entire response sequence by all participants" (Walker and Middleman 1988). The tabletop exercise is a versatile tool that can be applied to all phases of project management. The overarching benefit of tabletops is that they require people to pay attention both during development and as the system evolves (Walker and Middleman 1988).

One essential element to have in place for effective crisis management is a notification system. An effective notification system not only provides for contacting emergency response units, authorities, and key decision-makers, but also provides for accounting of personnel whereabouts and disposition. After the 1996 Atlanta Olympics bombing, a plan to track the whereabouts of United States (U.S.) athletes and officials was deployed within fifteen minutes of the blast (Lloyd 1996). Dick Schultz, executive director of the U.S. Olympic Committee, stated: "In a two-hour time span, we not only determined the location of everybody, we had them secured. We had put together a crisis management plan for as many situations as we needed to" (Lloyd 1996). Each U.S. athlete was issued a pager, the first time that this was ever done at an Olympics. The ability to account for all athletes and their whereabouts provides evidence for the effectiveness of their crisis plan.

Risk analysis, contingency planning, logic charts, and tabletop exercises represent several of the more common tools to help plan for crises in projects. Table 1 summarizes these tools by output. Project managers should think through their projects, in consultation with other project personnel, to select and use the tools judged to be most effective for the specific project. Once selected, these

Tool	Output
Risk Analysis	Identification of risks
Contingency Plan	Steps to take based on identified risks
Logic Chart	Specific steps to take in a crisis
Tabletop Exercise	Rehearse, discuss, and solidify a specific emergency response

Table 1 Summary of Crisis Planning Tools

tools should be developed and tested to ensure that people understand how to use them and what types of outcomes will result. Most certainly, any test of the tools results in refinement of the tools and learning on participants' behalf.

RECOMMENDATIONS FOR PROJECT MANAGERS

While we do not have a closed set of comprehensive strategies to offer other project managers to better plan for crises, we do have several recommendations to offer, based on experience in emergency management. Considering the uncertainty involved in crisis management, we would be wary of any closed set of strategies. Crisis management, by definition, is perplexing, constantly changing, full of uncertainties, and challenging to any manager—especially the project manager. Crisis planning logically parallels the uncertain nature of crisis management. Although there is no simple solution to the complex problems posed by crises, following are our recommendations.

■ Even for small projects, assign the job of developing at least a two-page risk analysis and contingency plan before the project begins. This is similar to a company appointing a manager of business interruption planning.

■ Assign the job of producing a notification sequence.

■ Use logic charts to design procedures that will not go awry during a crisis.

■ Use tabletop exercises because few people will look at a logic chart or even a procedure when a crisis occurs. Project managers will depend on what they have practiced, and this underscores the need and value of tabletops.

- Conduct these tabletop exercises quarterly to ensure readiness and to update procedures and responsibilities.
- Establish authority for crisis management before the crisis. The project manager is not always the best emergency manager, so choose the person who has the greatest knowledge of the operational issues associated with the crisis.
- Use emergency planning processes in projects, including risk analysis and contingency planning.
- Design effective, accurate, and timely feedback systems to provide early warning signs of failure and impending crises. A structured management process can help in focusing attention on regular tracking of relevant and critical indicators to surface the little problems before they become big ones. Become sensitive to indicators of impending project failure. Pay special attention to untracked indicators because these are the most likely to cause trouble. Develop antennae, and know when the project is going wrong.
- Choose a project manager indigenous to the country where the project is being conducted. An indigenous project manager will be sensitive to the social and political aspects of the project and its peripheral issues, and will catch more problems while they are small or otherwise undetectable to the outsider.
- Be mindful of the social and political consequences of crises or events. Critics, or stakeholders, bear significant influence on project success regardless of what the indicators of cost, schedule, and quality show. Learn how to satisfy stakeholders (Mallak, Patzak and Kurstedt 1991). Identify one spokesperson as a liaison with the public, and prepare a procedure for quick dissemination of information to all affected parties.
- Adopt a systems view and separate the crisis from the origin of the crisis. Consider the basic performance principles and problem-analysis techniques popularized in total quality management programs. Look forward and backward to assess the potential overall effects of the crisis.

These tools, recommendations, and strategies should help project managers to manage their crises better, and perhaps to avoid some crises altogether. Making time and resources available to those in charge of crisis planning is essential; otherwise, these critical tasks will be subordinated to the day-to-day activities, a vicious circle that can increase the likelihood of a larger crisis going undetected until it is too late. The regular and proper use and testing of risk analyses, contingency plans, logic charts, and tabletop exercises should surface the information, discussion of decisions and actions, and mitigation techniques that may reduce the occurrence and impact of crises in projects.

Acknowledgments

The preparation of this paper was partially funded by the United States Department of Energy Grant No. DE-FG05-86DP70033.

References

Bradford, M. 1996. Firms May Be Caught in a Five-Ring Circus: With Games on, Planning Will Pay off. *Business Insurance* (Feb. 2): 3.

Ceniceros, R. 1995. Nestle Resorts to Crisis. *Business Insurance* (Oct. 23): 83.

Gershanov, K. M. 1995. Emergency Preparedness in Five Easy Steps. *Occupational Health and Safety* 64.3: 51–53.

Kruse, C. 1993. Disaster Plan Stands Test of Hurricane. *Personnel Journal* (Jun.): 36–43.

Kurstedt, H. A., Jr., L. A. Mallak, and L. C. Pacifici. 1992. Expand Quality Management into the Customer's Environment to Establish Effective Measures and Standards. *Proceedings of the 1st International Symposium on Productivity and Quality Improvement* (Feb.): 478–85.

Lagadec, P. 1993. *Preventing Chaos in a Crisis.* London: McGraw-Hill.

Leonard, J. B. 1995. Assessing Risk Systematically: Illinois Power's Risk Assessment System. *Risk Management* 42.1: 12.

Lloyd, J. 1996. U.S. Official Says Athletes Were Safe—And Feel Safe. *USA Today* (Jul. 28): 3C.

Mallak, L. A., G. R. Patzak, and H. A. Kurstedt, Jr. 1991. Satisfying Stakeholders for Successful Project Management. *Computers and Industrial Engineering* 21 (Jul. 28): 429–33.

O'Connor, P. J. 1996. Security Practice for Convention Called a Success. *Chicago Sun-Times* (May 23): 23.

Sawle, W. S. 1991. Concerns of Project Managers: Crisis Project Management. *PM Network* 5.1: 25–29.

Slack, C. 1996. Bertha Gives VDOT Center Real-Life Situation to Test Computer System. *Richmond Times Dispatch* (Jul. 15): D–13.

Walker, J. A., and L. I. Middleman. 1988. Tabletop Exercise Programs Complement Any Emergency Management System. *Proceedings of the ANS Topical Meeting on Emergency Response—Planning, Technologies, and Implementation.* Charleston, South Carolina.

Avoiding Large-Scale Information Systems Project Failure: The Importance of Fundamentals

Erwin V. Martinez, CSC Consulting, Waltham, Massachusetts

Project Management Journal 25.2 (June 1994)

DURING THE PAST twenty years, business and government have experienced their fair share of large-scale information systems (IS) projects. And as anyone who has been involved in such efforts knows, a large-scale project is big in all measurable terms. Duration is measured in years, total team size numbers in the hundreds (or more), and work effort is tracked in tens of thousands of workdays. Furthermore, large-scale projects directly affect—and significantly alter—critical mainstream business functions. They therefore involve a broad cross-section of the business organization, uncover and address complex cross-functional issues, and fundamentally change core business operations.

Unfortunately however, large-scale projects are extremely difficult and challenging to manage—and frequently fall short of meeting their anticipated results. Consider the following real-life examples.

CASE #1: CITY GOVERNMENT

A large east-coast city engaged a major systems integration firm to completely replace the systems supporting the core business activities of one of its largest agencies. The systems were in a typical state of decay. They featured multiple, disjointed applications (some of which had been around for as long as twenty-five years) and data supported on disjointed data structures (some in formats no longer supported by their original vendors). And, as is common in such environments, enhancements became increasingly difficult to make, and some of the more recent requirements were impossible to support.

The systems integrator—known as a leader, particularly in large-scale project management—proposed a modern technical solution that included integrated databases and applications, a common user view, relational database technology, and CASE and repository tools for development. Originally scheduled for two to three years with a budget in the tens of millions of dollars, this project is years past its original completion date and is facing overruns of more than double the original estimate. Much to the displeasure of the city and agency involved, this project has already been featured in the computer industry trade press as a possible runaway project.

CASE #2: PUBLISHING COMPANY

A large, well-known publishing company decided to rethink the way it organizes its subscriber/customer information for customer service and marketing purposes. Reluctant to rely on outside vendors for project management, the company instead chose to give primary project management responsibility to internal managers—using vendors to supplement staff where numbers or specific skills were lacking. After approximately two years and millions of dollars in expenditures, the project was halted; project managers were replaced with newly hired, experienced managers; the IS department was reorganized; and the project was restarted. This resulted in, among other problems, continual delays and user management disenfranchisement.

CASE #3: MONEY CENTER BANK

In the late 1980s, a large bank developed and implemented software designed to significantly streamline and automate one of the bank's high-volume consumer-banking functions. Unfortunately, however, the bank was forced to shut the system down in the early 1990s because the software failed to meet its two primary goals. Instead of streamlining the function, the system failed to properly apply several business-processing rules to transactions (mainly because of programming errors and technical problems in data communications). In addition, users found that transactions that were supposed to take minutes instead took hours. An examination of the system's problems conducted well after its implementation revealed that the problems were readily recognizable and addressable through the use of common analysis, programming, and data communications practices and technologies—which, apparently, were not applied as the system was being designed and developed. As a consequence of this failure, the bank now finds its share of these customers' transactions diminished in comparison to its competition.

CASE #4: PUBLIC UTILITY

A medium-sized utility decided to develop new systems for all of its core business functions, including customer sales and service and work-order management. The company employed several systems integration firms, as well as a large force of its own employees, to work on the project. After approximately three years and $50 million had been invested, all the utility had to show for its efforts was a long series of delays and endless fingerpointing among the integration firms and the internal IS department. Faced with one delay too many, the utility stopped all development, reshuffled internal management, and hired one firm to re-estimate and resume the project. Although estimates vary, the system will eventually cost $50 million to $100 million more than expected, and *go live* four years later than planned.

CASE #5: STATE GOVERNMENT

A large state agency engaged a leading systems integration firm to develop and implement modern, online systems for its main business functions. This agency's operations are highly visible to the public, with offices located throughout the state. While development appeared to have gone well, problems began cropping up after the system was operating. The users discovered that the new system was too slow to serve normal customer traffic. (In most cases, customers were being serviced much more slowly than when they were using the old system.) The entire effort was a huge public-relations fiasco, as the local news media took the public officials and the systems integrator to task for their miscues. To remedy the situation, the agency was forced to use the old system until it made performance improvements to the new system. An official investigation later revealed that the performance problems were actually discovered by testing teams before implementation but, for reasons unknown, were ignored.

SUMMARY

In all of these cases, project failure was not a result of the use of *bleeding-edge* technologies or nontraditional or unproven methodologies. Nor was it because the individuals involved lacked sufficient industry or functional expertise, or because recalcitrant employees were somehow undermining the project to retain the existing system and old ways of doing business. The plain fact is that these projects failed because there was a breakdown in project management fundamentals.

Inattention to the fundamentals of project management will inevitably lead to project failure. This is especially true in more ambitious efforts, because large-scale projects allow little room to recover from fundamental mistakes. For instance, a delay of a month or two on a five-person project may be recoverable through increased staffing or overtime. However, a similar slowdown on a 300-person project has much more disastrous consequences. Likewise, alienation and distrust among six users are much easier to overcome than such feelings among 600 or 6,000 users.

Some industry professionals claim that the best way to avoid large-scale project failure is to simply stop doing large-scale projects.

This suggestion, however attractive, is impractical because it ignores a basic reality about corporate and government systems in the 1990s; that is, many organizations have allowed their information-processing capabilities to deteriorate so much that large-scale projects are imperative to their competitiveness—even their survival. Much in the way that large United States cities have allowed their physical infrastructures to deteriorate to a level of crisis, so have big business and government—either because of preoccupation with short-term profits or fear of large-scale change—delayed making investments in technology, thus allowing their information processing infrastructures to approach collapse.

As a result, large-scale projects are necessary to help these organizations make up for years of inadequate response to competitive pressures, customer demands, changing business conditions, and growing business volumes. Like it or not, large-scale projects will not go away.

BACK TO THE FUNDAMENTALS: PROJECT MANAGEMENT FUNCTIONS

To end this cycle of failure and improve the chances for project success, IS professionals must rededicate themselves to paying attention to the basic functions of project management, and must adopt methods to ensure that the essential project management functions are identified and earnestly performed. Toward this end, the following sections review these essential functions and their purposes, and outline a comprehensive approach to beginning a large-scale project that actively addresses these functions.

Essential Functions

Each large-scale project embraces a set of *essential functions* that must be actively performed for the project to be successful: executive, project, team, and analyst/doer (see Tables 1–4). The redundancy of stating that these functions must be "actively performed" is deliberate. Too often, functions are not actually performed, but addressed in name only. Perhaps they are merely appended to someone's job title, added to the duties of an already overloaded team or team member, or ignored outright by the people to whom they are assigned.

Function	Purpose	Effect on Project if Ignored
Strategic Business Decision-Making/ Policy Setting	Speak for the Business Sponsor the Project Serve as Ultimate Decision-Maker	Lack of Business Ownership
Strategic Business-Vision Guardian	Maintain Project's Focus on Enabling the Business Vision and Strategy	Becoming Irrelevant to the Business Loss of Support and Funding
Relationship Management	Maintain Cooperation of Business Community Communicate Project Issues and Status with Business Communicate Business Input to Project	Alienate Business Community Implement Solutions Unacceptable to the Business
Business Operations Expertise	Ensure Realistic Focus and Workable Solutions Interrogate Project Team for Completeness	Incomplete Business Solution Unplanned Rework
Devil's Advocate/ Creative Challenging	Challenging Ideas, Solutions and People to Achieve Excellence	Incomplete Business Solution Increased Mistakes and Unplanned Rework
Strategic IS Vision Guardian	Ensure Solution Is Consistent with IS Strategy Technical Solutions Alienation of IS community	Tendency Toward Uncoordinated, Unproven, and Mismatched
Detailed Project Oversight	Focus on Responsibility and Accountability Serve as Chief Project Executive	Unaccountable Project Out-of-Control Project
Quality Assurance	Build Quality into Solution Detect Quality Problems Ensure Follow-through to Remedy Quality Problems	Lack of Quality Rework
Contract Administration	Adhere to Agreed-upon Scope and Terms Make Only Explicit Changes to Scope and Terms	Incomplete Scope Incomplete Solution Legal Disputes
Legal Advisory	Stick to Solutions within Established Law and Regulation Ensure Timely Resolution of Legal Issues	Solutions That Violate Established Law and Regulation Rework Legal Disputes
Financial Control	Ensure Prudent Project Financial Planning	Unplanned Cost Overruns Incomplete Projects
Administrative Support Infrastructure	Enjoy Improved Level of Organization	Disorganization Resulting in Project Inefficiency and Poor Communications

Table 1   Executive Level Functions

Function	Purpose	Effect on Project if Ignored
Project Management	Conduct Detailed and Day-to-Day Management: — Anticipation — Planning — Oversight and Control — Data Collection and Reporting — Results Tracking and Response Analysis	Project Failure Disorganization Rework Poor Quality Missed Schedule Incomplete Solution Unworkable Solution
Systems Integration Architecture	Ensure Cohesive, Integrated, High-Quality, Workable Solution Coordinate Activities of Application, Data, and Technology Teams Take Holistic Perspective on Evolving Solution	Unworkable Solution Rework Poor Quality
Business Change Management	Ensure Business Acceptance of Solution Prepare Business for Entire Scope of Change	Business Rejection of Solution Solution Unworkable in Operation
Quality Assurance	Build Quality into Solution Detect Quality Problems Ensure Follow-through to Remedy Quality Problems	Lack of Quality Rework
Issue Management	Track and Resolve Business and Technology Issues	Delays Unworkable Solutions
Scope Control/ Change Control	Base Scope Control on Business Value	Incomplete Solution Delays Unworkable Solution
User Coordination and Relationship Management	Plan Well-Timed Involvement of User Experts and Decision-Makers Maintain User Cooperation and Good Will	Unworkable Solution Lack of Business Acceptance Unidentified Issues or Requirements Rework
IS Coordination and Relationship Management	Plan Well-Timed Involvement of Technical Experts and Decision-Makers Adhere to Standards Maintain IS Cooperation and Good Will	Unworkable Solution Lack of IS Acceptance Unidentified Technical Issues or Requirements Rework Lack of Adherence to Standards
Technical Configuration Administration	Coordinate Detail Aspects of Development Technical Environment Coordinate Build of Production Technical Environment	Delays Lost Work Unreliable Solution
Morale Officer	Maintain Project Team Morale Maintain Project Team Focus on Goals While Maintaining a Perspective Provide Communications Channel to Project Management and Project Executives on Morale Issues	Poor Morale Quality of Problems, Delays, etc., Resulting from Poor Morale
Administrative Support Infrastructure	Improve Level of Organization Improve Project Efficiency Improve Communications Conduct Detailed Administration of: — Project Control System — Library — Project Site Furniture and Equipment Logistics — Project Reports — Secretarial — Gofers	Disorganization Resulting in Project Inefficiency and Poor Communications

Table 2   Project Level Functions

Function	Purpose	Effect on Project if Ignored
Business-Process Redesign	Design Improvements to Architecture Business Work Flow, Taking Advantage of New Technology Achieve Work-Flow Efficiencies	Failure upon Implementation Unworkable Solution Incomplete Solution
Applications Architecture	Design Application Solution Resolve Interfacing Issues	Project Failure Unworkable Solution Incomplete Solution
Data Architecture	Design Data Solution	Project Failure Unworkable Solution Incomplete Solution
Technical Infrastructure Architecture	Design Production, Development, and Communications Technical Architecture	Project Failure Unworkable Solution Incomplete Solution
Facilities Architecture	Design Physical Work Space and Conditions in New Business Environment	Business Efficiencies Business Rejection of Solution
Knowledge Transfer Coordination	Ensure Orderly Transition of Specialized Knowledge and Skills from Project Team to Maintenance Personnel Manage Team Training	Failure after Implementation Unworkable Solution Incomplete Solution
Change Management Coordination	Develop Program to Introduce Business and System Change to the Business Cultivate Two-Way Communications with Business and Project	Business Rejection of Solution Unworkable Business Solution
Business Operations Expertise	Ensure Team's Analysis and Solutions Are Complete and Workable and Address Core Business Needs	Unworkable Solution
Quality Assurance	Build Quality into Solution Detect Quality Problems Ensure Follow-through to Remedy Quality Problems	Lack of Quality Rework
Team Leadership (typically, at Least one manager per major task)	Leadership for Specific Areas, Such as Programming, Integration Testing, etc.	Incomplete Solution Quality Problems Consistency Problems

Table 3   Team Level Functions

These essential functions are interdependent yet distinct, and define a complete framework that addresses all activities critical to a project's success. Ignoring, understaffing, de-emphasizing, or circumventing any of these functions invites failure.

Function	Purpose	Effect on Project if Ignored

Analysts and Doers	Get the Work Done
	Provide Analysts for Each Active
	   Architecture Area
	Provide Doers for Each Active
	   Architecture Area
		Project Failure
		Disorganization
		Rework
		Poor Quality
		Missed Schedule
		Incomplete Solution
		Unworkable Solution

Facilitation	Provide Expertise in the Conduct
	   of Effective Meetings
	Provide Expertise in the Identification
	   and Resolution of Issues
		Project Failure
		Disorganization
		Rework
		Poor Quality
		Missed Schedule
		Incomplete Solution
		Unworkable Solution

Quality Assurance	Build Quality into Solution Detect Quality Problems Ensure Follow-through to Remedy Quality Problems	Lack of Quality Rework

Business Operations Expertise	Ensure Team's Analysis and
	   Solutions Are Complete,
	   Workable, and Address Core
	   Business Needs at the Most
	   Detailed Level
		Unworkable Solution

Table 4 Analyst and Doer Functions

Recognition of these four levels is not an endorsement of the typical, hierarchical structure of organizations; it is merely an acknowledgment of stated reality. Because the prevailing structure of an organization will not change to accommodate a project—even a strategically critical one—successful project managers and team members must work within this structure.

Project management provides the structure that holds a project together up and down this hierarchy and across it to business and information technology constituencies (Figure 1). The essential functions at each level coordinate and manage the creative build of the end products, connect the team with its constituencies, and administer and control project processes.

The following sections contain more detailed discussions of the essential functions, their roles within a project, and some potential pitfalls that each function holds for project managers.

Executive-Level Functions

Organizations, like humans, are naturally averse to change. Thus, because large-scale projects involve a significant amount of change, companies tend to avoid engaging in them. However, while this *wait-and-see* attitude provides a certain level of comfort, it is also a formula for failure. Organizations must overcome this anxiety, and the only way they can do that is with active executive support and sponsorship. Top management's support of the effort helps motivate employees to get involved in the project and provides a measure of mental security to all involved.

In addition to contributing to a successful project launch, executive involvement and guidance helps ensure that the business vision is articulated and the project is managed toward attaining this vision. Without sufficient and substantive executive involvement, a large-scale project's focus frequently wavers, as the strategic business mission is supplanted by project or system objectives. A common example of loss of focus is when meeting an interim milestone date for finalizing the design becomes more important than designing a system that enables the organization to attain the business vision. In this scenario, the project team often takes shortcuts by performing incomplete analysis or leaving key and complex business issues unresolved. Unfortunately, while these actions may result in short-term *success* (i.e., meeting the design deadline), the system ultimately implemented likely will fail to meet the true business objectives.

As is evident in Table 1, several executive-level functions address the need to communicate frequently and comprehensively with business and IS constituencies not included in the project team, and to build and maintain positive relationships between all interested parties. This goes beyond ensuring technical adherence to a business mission or developing an information technology architecture strategy. Without active and willing participation by leaders within the organization that will inherit the system when the project is finished, building a workable solution is extremely difficult. Furthermore, regardless of how good the system is, it will often be rejected if key constituencies were ignored or alienated along the way.

In sum, executives must assume direct oversight of the project, managing the effort in much the same way that they oversee business operations and maintain P&L responsibility and accountability. They must ensure that a discipline of administration and

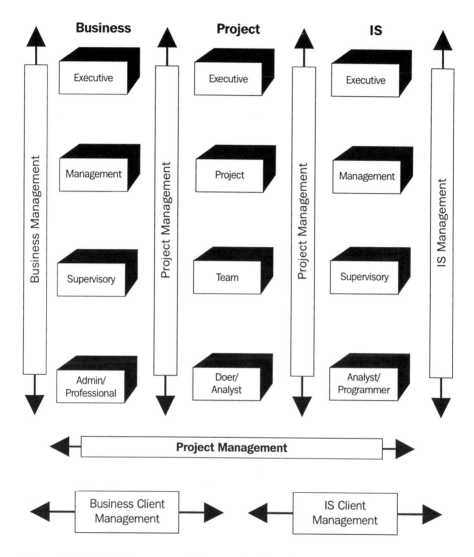

Figure 1   Project Management Communications Structure

controls is actively in place to plan, manage, and report on project activities, and they must help identify and resolve the most severe resource problems and business and technical issues. Ultimately, the responsibility for whether the project succeeds or fails rests with executive management.

Project-Level Functions

The traditional *stuff* of project management takes place on a projectwide basis, and it is these project-level functions that constitute the project manager's role. But, while these functions are generally handled by one person in small to midsize projects, the complexities of large-scale efforts require significantly more attention than can be provided by a single project manager. Therefore, it would not be improbable in very large projects for the eleven functions noted in Table 2 to be managed by more than eleven people. The advantage of this scenario is that it promotes the deployment of people with specialized skills to areas most appropriate to the use of those skills, thus avoiding the common pitfall of using essentially meaningless rules of thumb to gauge the number of projectwide roles; e.g., "We always take a solid IS manager and a full-time business manager and let them handle all projectwide activities."

For example, the skills needed by a project manager are much different than those required by the system architect.[1] A project manager must be adept at planning, controlling, orchestrating, and monitoring activities and resources, as well as at collecting information and building consensus. Technical skills, such as in-depth knowledge of the latest software packages and hardware platforms, are less important than the ability to direct team activities, track results, and anticipate potential roadblocks. Conversely, a system architect must be able to build creative business and technical solutions. Instead of focusing on the logistics and orchestration of the project, the architect is charged with identifying, designing, and assembling the correct combination of technical components that solve the business problems at hand. Because these tasks are fundamentally different in large projects and too consuming to combine, placing these responsibilities in the hands of a single person assuredly invites failure—not to mention burnout—on the part of the unfortunate individual.

An important distinction must be made, however, between recognizing the number and variety of projectwide functions and roles and diffusing responsibility from a single or small number of project managers. There should always be a focal point for project responsibility and accountability—whether it is a few leaders or a single person—so that there is no confusion about who is in charge and to whom those playing other projectwide roles must report.

Team-Level Functions

Large-scale projects operate as a set of focused and coordinated teams. The project management function delegates work in chunks to these teams and monitors the progress of each chunk. The systems-integration architecture function ensures that the chunks are coordinated into a holistic and feasible solution. The administrative-support function gives the teams logistical support and administers their project plans and clerical resources.

Two types of essential functions are prominent at the team level (Table 3). One type, which is guided by the systems integration architect, creatively plans and designs aspects of the developing business and systems solution, such as applications and business-process-redesign architecture. The other type manages and coordinates an aspect of solution delivery, such as change management or knowledge transfer coordination.

There are numerous potential pitfalls in managing team-level essential functions of which project managers must be aware. These include the following.

- Considering the project purely a technology effort and ignoring or deemphasizing business areas such as change management, process redesign, and facilities architecture.
- Diffusing responsibility for essential functions among several teams that have *system life-cycle* focuses. Examples of this are charging five to ten detail design and programming teams with resolving application and data-architecture concerns, or allowing every team to handle knowledge transfer.
- Abdicating management of team functions because they are *out of scope*. Large-scale projects implement broad, holistic change. Ignoring essential functions as *not my job* merely ensures the uncoordinated development of incomplete and perhaps unworkable solutions.
- Ignoring essential functions because "we never did it that way before." Large-scale projects are different. For example, in smaller projects it may not have been necessary to identify and empower an application architect role; however, ignoring this role in a large-scale project invites the development of a disjointed solution.

Analyst/Doer-Level Functions

No one would argue with the need to include people who actually get the work done (Table 4). However, organizations often overlook the criticality of managing the analyst/doer-level functions and resources that provide the keys to project success. For a large-scale project to be successful, managers cannot take for granted the people who do the work—because, usually, these *frontline* individuals are the first to encounter unexpected problems and have the most insightful suggestions for improvement.

To keep the effort on track, project managers must ensure that they provide realistic, well-scoped assignments to and maintain the continuity of personnel in this group throughout the project; make ongoing training in tools, techniques, and methods available to support the needs of project doers as they progress through their assignments; maintain morale and enthusiasm for the effort; coordinate the analysts' and doers' activities so they do not work at cross purposes; and facilitate quality two-way communication with this, the largest group within the project. Ignoring these issues significantly undermines the productivity of the project.

Some potential pitfalls in managing analyst/doer-level essential functions are as follows.

- Ignoring the need for specialized skills in favor of using the *bodies on hand*. A seemingly easy way out of difficult personnel decisions is to assign individuals on hand, and hope that they can grow into the position or learn while doing. This is a sure way to jeopardize mission-critical projects. Areas where this presents the most risk is in the need for expert facilitators, technology expertise, or business subject-matter experts.

- "Robbing Peter to pay Paul." Often, this can be as simple as double-counting people ("I know he's full-time technical support for the integration test, but can't he run the performance lab, too?") or ignoring team members' off-project responsibilities. Such activities clearly have a detrimental effect on work quality and timeliness, as well as on team member morale.

- Ignoring planning estimates. Some managers have a philosophy of understaffing to get the most out of their people. While this may keep the personnel costs to a minimum, it typically communicates to team members that management does not care enough about project quality to provide enough people to do the job (so cutting corners is acceptable). It also demonstrates a disregard for staff members' personal wellbeing and private time.

■ Deemphasizing *soft* skills. Because projects are not merely technical endeavors, it is perilous to ignore the need for good soft skills, such as business-client relation building, consensus building, facilitation, business writing, and listening. These skills are just as vital as those that are technically precise, like programming and data analysis. When the soft skills are missing or deemphasized, projects tend to alienate business clients and develop solutions that are uncoordinated or do not meet real business needs.

Because all of these large-scale project management functions are critical, undesirable consequences can result when any function is not performed (as is summarized in Tables 1–4). It is incumbent upon any project manager to recognize that because each consequence by itself can undermine the success of a large-scale effort, each function must be paid the respect it is due.

How to Achieve Large-Scale Project Success

With a clear understanding of the essential project management functions in hand, let us take a look at how this knowledge can be applied to help ensure the success of any large-scale project.

Because the ultimate goal is to substantially improve the success rate of large-scale projects, the best place to begin is in the initial phases of project planning. The following is an approach to starting large-scale projects that ensures that essential functions will be addressed and that cultural impediments will be identified and countered. Primary emphasis is placed on the approach's initial two steps—project scoping and planning, and assessing culture and values—as they have the greater impact on project success. These two steps should be performed concurrently. Also included is a brief discussion of other important steps that will facilitate successful large-scale project management.

Step 1: Project Scoping and Planning

Begin by scoping the project. Any of a dozen or so full life-cycle methodologies may be used to adequately scope and plan a large-scale project.[2] (Remember: Large-scale projects fail not because these methodologies are faulty, but because, in practice, fundamental and essential project management functions are ignored.) As all good methodologies dictate, scope should be defined upfront as completely as possible to ensure that all constituencies understand and agree to what is being undertaken.

Scoping should include a discussion of:

- business functions
- tangible and intangible benefits sought
- organizational areas affected
- major problems to be addressed
- major issues to be resolved during the project
- systems to be replaced
- technology goals and an outline of the target solution.

Throughout the scoping and planning process, confirm that the essential functions are addressed—both in the project organization and in work plan tasks. One way to do this is by conducting, with expert facilitation, a mid-point and final quality assurance review of the project plan. As all good quality-assurance programs require, the planners should walk through their plan and demonstrate that it is workable, that risks are identified, and that risk-mitigation techniques are employed. In addition, the project planners, executive sponsors, project managers, and other key players should be challenged to demonstrate that the essential functions will be performed. If particular individuals are going to be assigned key roles, they must have the requisite skills, experience, integrity, dedication, clout, and time availability. Everyone must recognize that skirting these issues during the planning stages only delays dealing with them until after the project is under way.

Finally, use organization charts to help illustrate the structure of the team and the accompanying reporting avenues.[3] While some companies may believe that organization charts are inherently too bureaucratic or formal, this is false. Avoiding the use of organization charts does not prevent the development of red tape; instead, it creates the potential to overlook the assignment of essential management functions. Whether a project is run in a bureaucratic manner depends on the styles of the project executives and managers—not on the existence of an organization chart.

Step 2: Culture and Values Assessment

Successful businesses tend to have organization cultures that are strategically appropriate and adaptable to change.[4] Given the amount of change introduced both by the existence of a large project team and the implementation of large-scale change, this is likely also true for successful large-scale projects. For large-scale projects, every effort should be made to ensure that the organization's culture is compatible for the magnitude of change being introduced.

The second step, therefore, involves conducting a culture and values assessment of all sponsoring and affected business units, as well as of the IS organization.[5] The goal of the assessment is to gauge the organization's current culture and its fit with the change to be introduced by both the new project and the implementation of its solution. Due to the sensitive nature of such an activity and the potential for bias, it will likely be necessary to use an objective third party to conduct this assessment.

The end products of the assessment should include:

- identification and analysis of the pervasive cultures and values in the organization
- analysis of the characteristics of cultures and values that are appropriate for successful implementation of the level of change to be encountered during and after the project
- outline of a change management plan to gradually move the organization toward behaviors consistent with the changes to be introduced by the successful large-scale projects.

Anyone who has worked in large organizations will readily understand that a culture assessment and change management plan will not result in a rapid change in organizational behaviors and reward systems or in deeply held principles and values. Changing the core values and behaviors of large groups of people is a slow, difficult, and tricky process. However, assessment and change plans can help organizations begin to understand and adjust their cultures to be more receptive to change. Such plans help explain to individuals the attitudes and behaviors that they must learn and adopt to succeed. Being aware that the organization is embracing new ways of doing business will help empower people to break out of the old behavior patterns.

For large-scale projects with the broadest reach, the culture and values assessment may require a review of the entire business organization. In this case, the assessment should be conducted under the aegis of the most senior executives sponsoring the project. Without their active involvement and support, such a broad and sensitive effort will surely fail. Indeed, any cynicism or lack of seriousness about the role of organizational cultures in large-scale projects will quickly be felt by the organization as a whole, which would help to undermine any conclusions the assessment eventually reaches.

These two steps may also be used in a project that is already under way. In particular, those assuming responsibility for the executive-level detailed project oversight and quality assurance functions may find the tables in this article useful as checklists for ensuring that no essential functions are being slighted or ignored. Furthermore, the cultural and values assessment can be used in a project in progress because it is never too late to identify and adjust cultures and values that could impede the effort's success.

Other Steps

Several other steps must also be taken to help a large-scale project succeed.

- Articulate the business vision, and document it and the project's role in achieving the vision. Use this to generate a greater understanding of the project's true goals and to establish the scope of the business goals.
- Develop a communications plan that executes the functions of relationship management and IS coordination.
- Ask executive management to articulate its oversight goals and begin to define its most important project success measurements/anticipated benefits. This will enable project managers to build a plan that meets the executives' information needs.
- Establish tracking systems (usually on microcomputer-based software) for legal issues, project issues, quality assurance points, and scope-change management. The tracking systems should manage the items through a life cycle that includes steps such as initiation, fact finding, analysis, disposition, incorporation, and closure. During the life cycle, responsibility and accountability should be explicitly defined for each item.

- Establish project management software with the project master plan's tasks, budgets, assignments, milestones, and schedules.
- Develop an administrative support/logistics plan. For large-scale projects, the logistics of obtaining computers, establishing LANs, securing work space, and staffing the project team can be quite extensive.
- Develop a concept or baseline solution in those cases where the concept of the end-state solution is definable. Often, with large-scale IS projects, a baseline design concept is needed to begin the systems architecture coordination.
- Conduct a preliminary project-team skills and training needs analysis. When managing very large teams, it is best to anticipate and plan for training in new technologies, techniques, or methodologies as early as possible. The logistics for arranging and scheduling the training can be daunting.
- Develop a quality assurance plan. Large-scale projects usually require dedicated quality assurance team members. This plan is, in effect, the quality assurance team members' own project plan.
- Develop a business-user-expert-contact matrix. Identify the business user experts upon whom the project team will rely for expertise, issue analysis and resolution, and sign-off. Large-scale IS projects require cross-organization participation and decision-making. It will take some time for the business managers to sort through these roles and assignments.

THE CHALLENGE OF LARGE-SCALE PROJECTS

The high incidence of failure among large-scale projects is a huge threat to modern commercial and government organizations. Technology innovations, expanding markets, increased regulation, growing customer demands, and new sources of competition are rapidly changing the business environment. Government is straining to expand its scope and volume of services while reining in costs. Information technology represents a source of power that, if properly managed, can enable organizations to meet these challenges. But, while the opportunities presented by information technology are unmatched in world history, our frequent inability to manage the introduction of solutions that significantly leverage technology is standing in the way of our capitalizing on these opportunities.

The solution to large-scale project management lies within our grasp. We must get better at executing what we already know, at applying our expertise and skills. We must rework our organizational cultures so that they more readily accommodate change. And we must never forget that mastering and applying the fundamentals is key to successful large-scale IS project management.

Notes

1. This is an instance of the differentiation between "technical or industry body of knowledge" and "project management body of knowledge," as described in the Project Management Institute's *A Guide to the Project Management Body of Knowledge* (*PMBOK® Guide*) framework.
2. Information systems' full life-cycle development methodologies are referred to here. The better of such methodologies would normally include most of the types of definitions and practices included in the *PMBOK® Guide* discussions of the framework and scope functions.
3. Of course, organization charts themselves do not ensure successful projects. However, large-scale projects are particularly in need of organizational clarity. See, for example, *Building Quality Software*, Robert L. Glass, Prentice-Hall Inc., 1992, or "ownership of quality responsibility" in the *PMBOK® Guide* discussion of the quality function.
4. This widely held view was recently supported by research documented in *Corporate Culture and Performance*, John P. Kotter and James L Heskett, The Free Press, 1992.
5. The assessment of culture and values should include the analysis of the role of processes, such as the administration of compensation and evaluation and behavioral aspects of team members as they are defined in the *PMBOK® Guide* discussion of the human resources management function.
6. The scope of the communications plan for large-scale IS projects would be equivalent to that of the communications management function of the *PMBOK® Guide*.

An Analysis of Cost Overruns on Defense Acquisition Contracts

David S. Christensen, Air Force Institute of Technology, Wright-Patterson
Air Force Base

Project Management Journal 24.3 (Sept. 1993)

> The statements made in this article are those of the author,
> and do not represent the position of the Air Force Institute
> of Technology, the United States Air Force, the Department
> of Defense, or any other government agency.

DONALD J. YOCKEY, the former Under Secretary of Defense for Acquisition, has called for more realism in the defense acquisition process (1991, 35). More specifically, he has called for more realistic cost estimates. The hope is that more realistic estimates will help surface problems in enough time to resolve them.

Based on a review of over five hundred contracts, the Office of the Under Secretary of Defense for Acquisition (OUSD(A)) has observed that once a contract is 15 percent complete, it is highly unlikely to recover from a cost overrun (Abba 1992). Despite this important observation, contractor and government personnel often claim that their programs are different.

This article examines the history of cost overruns reported on sixty-four completed defense contracts. Its purpose is to formally test the observation of OUSD(A). Results confirm the observation at the 95 percent level of confidence and were generally insensitive to the contract type (price, cost), the contract phase (development, production), the type of weapon system (air, ground, sea), and the armed forces service (air force, army, navy) that managed the contract. After a review of terminology, concepts, and related research for those unfamiliar with the area, the methodology, results, and managerial implications are described.

BACKGROUND

Gansler reports that the average cost overrun on defense acquisition contracts is 40 percent (1989, 4). Cost data on defense contracts are regularly reported on cost management reports prepared by defense contractors. These reports include the cost performance report (CPR) and the cost/schedule status report. Department of Defense Instruction 5000.2 requires the CPR on all contracts judged significant enough for cost/schedule control systems criteria (C/SCSC). Significant contracts are research, evaluation, test, and development contracts with estimated costs of $60 million or more, or procurement contracts with estimated costs of $250 million or more (1991, 11B2]. Thus, a 40 percent cost overrun on a procurement contract that barely qualifies as significant is at least $100 million dollars!

The cost/schedule control systems criteria are not a system. Instead, they are minimal standards for contractors' internal management control systems. The purpose of the criteria is to foster reliable decision-making by contractor and government personnel. One of the requirements is that data reported by the contractor be summarized from the same systems that the contractors use for internal management. These and other requirements help ensure that the data submitted to the government is useful for decision-making.

Another requirement of the criteria is a disciplined budgeting system. A time-phased budget of all the authorized work on the contract—termed the *performance measurement baseline*—is developed by the contractor. The baseline is simply the summation of budgets assigned to elements of work on the contract. Because each element of work has a schedule, the budget for the work is said to be *time phased*.

The time-phased budgets assigned to work elements—termed the *budgeted cost of work scheduled* (BCWS), form the basis for earned value measurement and reporting. Earned value—also termed the *budgeted cost of work performed* (BCWP)—is the same number as BCWS. The only difference is when they are recorded; BCWS is recorded when work is planned to be accomplished, and BCWP is recorded when work is actually accomplished. If work is accomplished at a time different than it is planned to be accomplished, then a schedule variance is identified. In a disciplined budgeting system, all significant variances are investigated in a timely manner.

A schedule variance often signals a cost variance. A cost variance is simply the difference between the BCWP and the actual cost of the same work, termed actual cost of work performed (ACWP). As with the schedule variance, the criteria require the timely investigation and reporting of significant cost variances. The intent is that through the timely analysis of variances, problems will be corrected before they become serious.

Figures 1 and 2 illustrate the relationship between the three basic data elements just described. The performance measurement baseline is the cumulative expression of BCWS. Against this baseline, performance (BCWP) and actual cost (ACWP) are measured. Figure 1 illustrates the typical condition of defense contracts: over budget and behind schedule.

In this article, the focus is on cost overruns. A cost overrun is an adverse cost variance. Figure 1 illustrates two kinds of cost overruns, termed the *current overrun* and the *overrun at completion*. The current overrun is the adverse cost variance to date. The overrun at completion is the difference between the total budget for all the work on the contract, termed the *budget at completion* (BAC) and the estimated final cost of the contract, termed the *estimate at completion"* (EAC). Note that the overrun at completion is an estimate until the contract is completed. As shown in Figure 2, at the end of the contract, BCWP equals BCWS, and the current overrun is the final overrun.

The EAC is an important number and is very controversial, largely because there is literally an infinite number of possible EAC formulas (Christensen et al. 1992; (Department of the Air Force 1989). The criteria do not prescribe a particular formula or set of formulas; the choice lies with the contractor. The only requirement is that the estimate be rational (Department of the Air Force 1987).

Because rational people can disagree, the government will usually evaluate the reasonableness of the contractor's estimate by computing a range of EACs. Unfortunately, there is little guidance on what constitutes a reasonable range. As a result, the projected

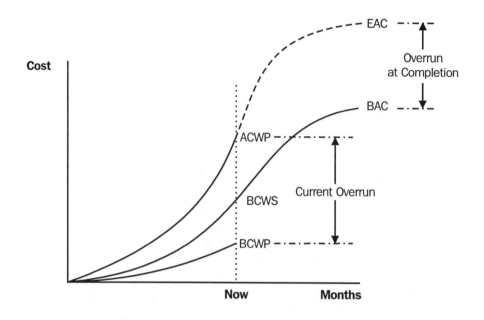

Figure 1 The Current Cost Overrun and Overrun at Completion

overrun at completion supported by the government program office is usually higher than the contractor's estimate. Because the government program office is necessarily an advocate of its program (Welch 1991), its estimate may also be unrealistically optimistic.

One way to assess the reasonableness of the estimated overrun at completion is to compare it to the overrun to date. If the overrun at completion is less than the overrun to date, then the contractor or program office is optimistically projecting a cost recovery. Such was the case in the A-12 program.

In April of 1990, the A-12 was in full-scale development and was 37 percent complete (Beach 1990). The contractors' reported overrun at completion was $354 million. The overrun to date was $459 million (Campbell and Fleming 1991). Thus, the A-12 contractors were predicting a recovery of $105 million. Although this may seem optimistic, it is impossible to know for sure, because the A-12 was canceled in January of 1991.

Is such optimism justified? More specifically, is it unrealistically optimistic for the predicted overrun at completion to be less than

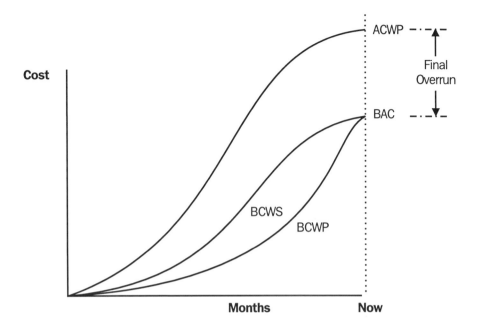

Figure 2 The Final Cost Overrun

the overrun to date? Based on a review of cost-overrun data on completed contracts, the answer is that such optimism is unrealistic with 95 percent confidence.

WHAT PRIOR RESEARCH SAYS

There has been some research into this issue. Abba and Christle, senior analysts at the Office of the Under Secretary of Defense for Acquisition (OUSD(A)), have observed:

> Given a contract is more than 15 percent complete, the [final] overrun at completion will not be less than the overrun to date, and the [final] percent overrun at completion will be greater than the percent overrun to date. (Abba 1992)

This observation is based on a review of cost data on over five hundred completed contracts. The analysts are quick to point out, however, that timely management attention to adverse cost variances can reverse them, especially early in the program. The problem has been a failure to use performance measurement data proactively.

The assertion of Abba and Christle is based on a casual review of over five hundred completed contracts. The results of two empirical studies support the assertion (Christensen and Payne 1992; Heise 1991). Both studies established that once a contract is 20 percent complete, the cumulative cost performance index (CPI) does not change by more than 10 percent; in fact, in most cases, it only worsens. (For example, in April 1990, the A-12 program was 37 percent complete and reported a CPI of 0.77. By September, the program was 47 percent complete and its CPI was 0.72.)

As shown in Equation 1, the CPI is a ratio of BCWP to ACWP.

CPI = BCWP/ACWP   [Equation 1]

A CPI that is less than 1 means that for every dollar spent, less than one dollar of work is accomplished. It follows that when the cumulative CPI is less than 1, the contract is experiencing a cost overrun, and because an unfavorable cumulative CPI only worsens, a contract is not likely to recover from a cost overrun. Therefore, if the predicted overrun at completion is less than the overrun to date, the contractor's estimated final cost of the contract (EAC) is unrealistically optimistic. This study further establishes these results by examining the cost overrun history on sixty-four completed contracts extracted from the Defense Acquisition Executive Summary (DAES) database.

METHODOLOGY

The DAES database has received summary data on completed contracts since 1977 (Christle 1981). Presently, data are summarized from cost performance reports by government program offices and sent to OUSD(A) as quarterly DAES Reports (Department of Defense 1991). The database is a fairly detailed source of information on the cost performance of the country's defense-acquisition contracts. It is also reasonably accurate because most of the contracts in the database are C/SCSC compliant.

For this study, a sample of sixty-four completed contracts was extracted from the database. Although the sample was purely judgmental, it is considered sufficiently rich to generalize to any C/SCSC-

Contract		Overrun ($ Millions)			Overrun (Percent)		
Category	Number	Avg	Min	Max	Avg	Min	Max
All	64	36	-3	493	18	-3	109
Army	28	21	-3	46	20	-3	46
Air Force	18	49	-2	407	19	-1	109
Navy	18	47	0	493	13	0	46
Air	43	45	-3	492	18	-3	109
Ground	13	23	7	42	21	5	45
Sea	8	12	0	36	12	0	38
Development	25	38	-2	407	21	-1	109
Production	39	35	-3	493	16	-3	46
Cost	23	41	-2	493	14	-1	46
Price	41	34	-3	407	20	-3	109

Table 1 Final Cost Overrun on Sixty-four Completed Contracts

compliant defense contract. Table 1 summarizes final cost overrun data by various categories considered relevant to this study.

Based on the OUSD(A) assertion and the results of prior research, four hypotheses were tested (Table 2). For Hypothesis 1, the average final cost overrun in dollars (FCO$) exceeds the average cost overrun to date (CO$). Hypothesis 2 is the same, except the overruns are expressed in percentages. If these hypotheses are correct with statistical significance, then recoveries from cost overruns are improbable with a certain level of confidence. For this study, the hypotheses were tested at the 95 percent level of confidence.

Based on the results of prior research involving estimates at completion (Christensen et al. 1992), it was expected that the results of the testing may be sensitive to the contract completion point and other factors specific to the contracts in the sample. Therefore, the hypotheses were systematically tested at nine contract completion points (ten to 90 percent at 10 percent increments) for various categories within the sample. The categories examined were the contract type (fixed price, cost), the contract phase (development, production), the generic type of weapon system (air, ground, sea), and the armed forces service that managed the contract (air force, army, navy).

The remaining hypotheses are related to the results of the referenced CPI stability studies, which established that the cumulative CPI tends to worsen from the 20 percent completion point. Here,

Hypothesis	Interpretation
H1: FCO$ > CO$	Recoveries from Cost Overruns ($) Are Improbable
H2: FCO% > CO%	Recoveries from Cost Overruns (%) Are Improbable
H3: ß$ > 0	Cost Overruns ($) Tend to Increase
H4: ß% > 0	Cost Overruns (%) Tend to Increase

Table 2 Hypotheses

the hypothesis was that the average cost overrun tended to increase. To test this hypothesis, the average cost overrun (CO) was regressed against percent complete (x):

$$CO = \alpha + \beta x \qquad \text{[Equation 2]}$$

If the resulting slope coefficient (Michelle, see text of article for this symbol) is positive with statistical significance, then the hypothesis is accepted, which means that cost overruns tend to increase. In Hypothesis 3, the average cost overrun was in dollars; in Hypothesis 4, the average cost overrun was a percent. As with hypotheses 1 and 2, hypotheses 3 and 4 were tested on the entire sample and on various categories of the sample.

Equations 3 and 4 define the current cost overrun and final cost overrun in dollars. Equations 5 and 6 define the overruns as percentages.

$$\text{Current Overrun (CO\$)} = \text{Cum ACWP} - \text{Cum BCWP} \qquad \text{[Equation 3]}$$

$$\text{Final Overrun (FO\$)} = \text{Final ACWP} - \text{BAC} \qquad \text{[Equation 4]}$$

$$\text{Current Overrun Percent} = 100*(\text{CO\$/Cum BCWP}) \qquad \text{[Equation 5]}$$

$$\text{Final Overrun Percent} = 100*(\text{FO\$/BAC}) \qquad \text{[Equation 6]}$$

The cost overruns were averaged for each category of the sample by dividing the number of contracts in that category into the total overrun for that category. The averaging was done at various stages of completion ranging from 10 to 100 percent complete, where percent complete was defined as follows:

$$\text{Percent Complete} = 100*(\text{Cum BCWP/BAC}) \qquad \text{[Equation 7]}$$

Data earlier than the 10 percent completion point were not considered sufficiently reliable. It can take as long as one year from contract award for the contractor to demonstrate C/SCSC compliance. Until then the data on the cost performance report are suspect.

RESULTS

As shown in the remaining tables, the hypotheses were generally confirmed at the 95 percent level of confidence. Table 3 shows the results of testing hypotheses 1 and 2 on the entire sample of sixty-four contracts. Recoveries from cost overruns expressed in either dollars or as a percentage are improbable, especially cost overruns experienced between the 10 to 70 percent completion points. Between these points, the difference between the final cost overrun and the overrun to date was statistically significant at confidence levels well above 95 percent. After the 70 percent completion, the current overrun percent is necessarily much closer to the final overrun percent, because monthly expenditures typically decrease as the work nears completion.

Hypotheses 1 and 2 were also generally confirmed for the categories of the sample examined. In short, *recoveries from cost overruns on defense contracts are highly improbable, regardless of the contract's type, the contract's phase, the type of weapon system, or the armed forces service that managed the contract.* (Supporting tables that document these results are not provided here but are available from the author.)

Table 4 shows the results of testing hypotheses 3 and 4, and confirm that *cost overruns on defense contracts tend to increase.* The slope coefficients were greater than zero with statistical significance for the entire sample and for each category of the sample that was examined.

MANAGERIAL IMPLICATIONS

The results of this research show that recoveries from cost overruns on defense contracts are highly improbable and that cost overruns tend to worsen as a defense contract proceeds to completion. This was found to be true regardless of the type or phase of the contract, the type of weapon system, or the armed forces service that managed the contract. The results are consistent with the results of related research involving the stability of the CPI and confirm the

	Cost Overrun ($ Millions)				Cost Overrun (Percent)			
PC	CO	FO-CO	SD	t	CO	FO-CO	SD	t
10	2.6	33.6	76.3	3.53	5.5	12.4	20.7	4.78
20	3.8	32.4	73.5	3.53	7.8	10.0	20.6	3.88
30	5.3	30.9	73.3	3.38	10.0	7.8	19.2	3.26
40	9.3	27.0	60.6	3.57	9.8	8.0	15.9	4.04
50	14.0	22.2	53.8	3.30	11.9	5.9	14.9	3.18
60	18.3	17.9	45.2	3.17	13.2	4.6	12.3	3.02
70	23.6	12.7	38.9	2.61	14.7	3.1	11.1	2.21
80	30.1	6.2	26.9	1.84	16.5	1.3	9.4	1.10
90	35.9	0.3	1.5	1.84	17.6	0.2	1.7	1.12
100	36.3	0.0	—	—	17.8	—	—	—

PC = Percent Complete; CO = Current Overrun; FO = Final Overrun; SD = Standard Deviation; t = t Statistic; $t_{\alpha = .05, df = 63} = 1.645$

Table 3   Recovery from Cost Overruns Is Improbable (All Contracts)

observations of senior analysts at the Office of the Under Secretary of Defense for Acquisition.

These results have strong managerial implications for the project manager: More realistic projections of the final costs are needed. When the projected overrun at completion is less than the overrun to date, the projected overrun at completion is too optimistic. Former Under Secretary of Defense for Acquisition Donald J. Yockey commented on this issue:

> We can't afford to understate, sit on, or cover up problems in any program—at any time—at any level. They must be brought forward. This includes not just "show stoppers" but also "show slowers." I can't stress this strongly enough. (1991, 26)

Without more realistic estimates, senior management may be lulled into a false sense of security about its programs and fail to take appropriate action to correct problems.

Wayne Abba and Gary Christle, senior analysts at the Office of the Under Secretary of Defense for Acquisition, have commented that although recoveries from cost overruns are improbable, they

Contract	Cost Overrun ($ Millions)			Cost Overrun (Percent)		
Categories	Slope (β)	SE	t	Slope (β)	SE	t
All	0.325	0.020	16.13	0.198	0.009	22.09
Army	0.186	0.013	14.27	0.234	0.016	15.08
Air Force	0.407	0.034	12.11	0.180	0.005	36.11
Navy	0.459	0.021	21.38	0.159	0.013	12.20
Air	0.416	0.022	18.71	0.210	0.010	20.30
Ground	0.168	0.024	7.06	0.193	0.018	11.00
Sea	0.095	0.008	12.57	0.139	0.013	10.37
Development	0.318	0.024	13.37	0.232	0.008	29.12
Production	0.330	0.019	17.18	0.176	0.012	15.08
Cost	0.393	0.018	21.40	0.166	0.015	10.88
Price	0.287	0.022	12.93	0.215	0.006	34.48

SE = Standard Error of Slope Coefficient with the Intercept Forced to Zero; t = t statistic; $t_{\alpha = .05, df = 8}$ = 1.895

Table 4 Cost Overruns Tend to Increase

are possible, especially if management pays proper attention to them. With proper attention, adverse variances have been reversed.

Proper attention requires a timely and disciplined analysis of variances as they are identified. It also requires a proper culture. A *shoot-the-messenger* culture was partly responsible for the delayed reporting of adverse information on the A-12 program (Beach 1990). Accordingly, senior management should make every effort to cultivate a healthy attitude regarding variance reporting. Managers are necessarily advocates of their projects. But, this does not mean suppressing or delaying the communication of adverse information about their projects to senior decision-makers.

It is not known if recoveries from cost overruns on nondefense projects are also improbable. Perhaps, additional research can explore this issue. Technical and political problems that contribute to cost overruns on defense projects may not be relevant to nondefense projects; however, the shoot-the-messenger culture involved in the A-12 program is certainly a potential problem in nondefense industries.

A related *cultural* factor that contributed to the cancellation of the A-12 was the natural optimism of senior management. In testimony before Congress, Navy Secretary of Defense Garrett characterized the senior managers involved in the A-12 program as "can do" people who did not admit to failure lightly (Ireland 1991). Although optimism has its place, it can be dangerous when it blinds the manager to the truth.

Finally, social scientists have extensively documented many real-world examples of "escalation error" (Staw 1981; Staw and Ross 1986). In these examples, the decision-maker is extremely reluctant to cancel an ongoing project or switch to an alternative despite excessive overruns or other compelling evidence that the project has failed or that the alternative is superior to the present course of action. In some cases, the manager chooses to escalate commitment to the project by increasing the spending on the project. Researchers (Staw 1981; Staw and Ross 1986) have attributed such behavior to psychological factors, such as a myopic "can do" attitude or a need to "save face." More recently, others (Chandra et al. 1989) have suggested that escalation error is caused by the manager's desire to protect his reputation in the managerial labor market. Given the adverse economic consequences of cost overruns, additional research in this area is needed.

References

Abba, Wayne. Program Analyst. 1992. Interview. Office of the Under Secretary of Defense (Acquisition), Washington, DC.

Beach, Chester Paul, Jr. 1990. A-12 Administrative Inquiry. Report to the Secretary of the Navy. Department of the Navy, Washington, DC.

Campbell, Dennis G., and Quentin W. Fleming. 1991. The A-12 Program Management Summary. Presentation by Wayne Abba at NSIA/MSS meeting at Los Angeles, California.

Chandra, Kanoida, Robert Bushman, and John Dickhaut. 1989. Escalation Errors and the Sunk Cost Effect: An Explanation Based on Reputation and Information Asymmetries. *Journal of Accounting Research* 27 (Spring): 59–77.

Christensen, David S. 1989. Management Control Systems Theory and Cost/Schedule Control Systems Criteria. *National Estimator* (Fall): 29–34.

Christensen, David S., and Kirk Payne. 1992. Cost Performance Index Stability—Fact or Fiction? *Journal of Parametrics* 10 (Apr.): 27–40.

Christensen, David S., Richard C. Antolini, and John McKinney. 1992. A Review of Estimate at Completion Research. *Cost Estimating and Analysis—Balancing Technology and Declining Budgets* (Jul.): 207–24.

Christle, Gary L. 1981. Automation of Program/Project Cost Reports Within DOD. *National Estimator* 1 (Spring): 22–27.

Department of the Air Force. 1987. *Cost/Schedule Control Systems Criteria Joint Implementation Guide.* Washington, DC: Headquarters Air Force System Command.

———. 1989. *Guide to Analysis of Contractor Cost Data.* Air Force System Command Pamphlet 173-4. Washington, DC: Headquarters Air Force System Command.

Department of Defense. 1991. *Defense Acquisition Management Policies and Procedures.* Department of Defense Instruction 5000.2. Washington, DC.

Gansler, Jacques S. 1989. *Affording Defense.* Cambridge, Massachusetts: The MIT Press.

Heise, Capt. Scott R. 1991. A Review of Cost Performance Index Stability. MS Thesis, AFIT/GSM/LSY/91S-12. School of Systems and Logistics, Air Force Institute of Technology, Wright-Patterson Air Force Base, Ohio.

Ireland, Andy. 1991. The A-12 Development Contract: A Blueprint for Disaster. Remarks to the Institute of Cost Analysis Washington Area Chapter, 12 December 1990. *Newsletter of the Society of Cost Estimating and Analysis* (Oct.): 26–27.

Staw, Barry M. 1981. The Escalation of Commitment to a Course of Action. *Academy of Management Review* 6: 577–87.

Staw, Barry M., and J. Ross. 1986. Behavior in Escalation Situations: Antecedents, Prototypes, and Solutions. In *Research in Organizational Behavior.* Eds. S. Cummings and B. Staw. Greenwich, Conn.: JAI Press.

Welch, J. J., Jr., Assistant Secretary of the Air Force (Acquisition). 1991. Program Advocacy. Acquisition Policy Letter 91M-005 (Apr. 8).

Wilson, Brian D. 1991. An Analysis of Contract Cost Overruns and Their Impacts. Masters Thesis, AFIT/GCA/ LSY/92S-8. Air Force Institute of Technology, Ohio.

Yockey, Donald J. 1991. Keynote speech given at the C/SCSC National Workshop at Falls Church, Virginia, 28 Oct. 1991. *National Estimator* (Winter): 35–38.

Project Monitoring for Early Termination

Jack Meredith, University of Cincinnati

Project Management Journal 19.5 (Nov. 1988)

PROJECT MANAGEMENT CONTINUES to play an ever-larger role in society and industry. As consumers' demands for more unique products and services increase while the corresponding life cycles of those products and services decrease, the need for management through project organization escalates. With this increasing importance of successful projects, more attention has been focused on the managerial aspects of project management, and particularly on those approaches that promise higher project payoffs or more successful projects.

The number of articles on how to better manage projects has increased significantly in the last decade. Such articles now appear in journals and magazines in fields from engineering to sociology (Meredith and Mantel 1985). Unfortunately, not all projects are successful. Yet, very little has been written about identifying failing projects and terminating them. Furthermore, most of what has been written has concerned the field of research and development (R&D), rather than projects in general (Balachandra and Raelin 1980; Buell 1967; Dean 1968; Tadisina 1986).

Yet, the importance of quickly terminating a failing project can hardly be overemphasized. Stewart has noted the exponential increase in cost to cut time from a project as the project nears completion (1965). Similarly, sunk costs accumulate rapidly as termination of a failing project is delayed. Through early termination, the organization can save not only the future costs of the project but also the time, effort, and organizational disruption of a project failure. Guidelines for recognizing upcoming project failure and implementing an early termination, if it is justified, are just as important as guidelines for successfully managing projects in the first place.

This article discusses the difficulty of early project termination and why it has so often been unsuccessful. An early termination-monitoring system is then described, which offers promise in rectifying some of these problems.

EARLY PROJECT TERMINATION

Early project termination (EPT) may be considered as the cessation of activity with abandonment of the project. Typically, this would occur when the costs and disadvantages of continuing the project were judged to outweigh the benefits and advantages of project completion. Dean surveyed a number of executives to determine the actual reasons for EPT of R&D projects in their firms, and he found that the main reasons were the low probabilities of achieving the technical objectives of the projects or commercializing the results with an adequate return on investment (1968).

Buell, in an early effort, provided some managerial guidelines for discontinuing R&D projects that were likely to become failures (1967). He developed an extensive set of questions that managers should consider during the progress of their firms R&D projects, because it was so difficult to specify solid standards for the EPT decision. His list included items ranging from the viability of the project concept itself to changes in the direction of the firms strategy.

Meredith identified a number of factors that computer-implementation projects required for successful continuation (1981). These factors were divided into three major categories: technical, processes, and inner-environmental issues. Of major interest here is the last category, which comprises two primary factors. The first is the continuing importance of the project to the organization. In particular, it must be a *current* problem that the project is addressing. The problem may be either one of cost or opportunity, but substantial resources must be already committed, or about to be, to addressing it. The second factor is the willingness of management to make the organizational and managerial changes required to utilize the project results.

More recently, Balachandra and Raelin offered a list of ten quantitative and thirteen qualitative factors that could be scored to decide whether to terminate particular R&D projects (1980). As with Buell, their lists included project viability and other related factors. The advantage of their approach, however, is its formality and rigor. Systematic analysis should improve the ability of managers to make correct EPT decisions, particularly as experience is gained with the process.

Tadisina's research used factors such as those of Balachandra and Raelin in a statistical-discriminant analysis to predict project success or failure (1986). His database consisted of 274 questions posed to managers of twenty-one firms in four major industries concerning the success or failure of 220 R&D projects. Factor analysis of the responses resulted in the isolation of twenty-three major factors grouped in five categories. If disaggregated by industry type, predictions of success and failure were significantly more accurate than prediction in general, ranging from over 70 percent to almost 90 percent.

In spite of such progress, it has too frequently been the case that projects were allowed to continue well past the time when it was obvious that they were headed for disaster. More recent research has now developed some insight into reasons for such behavior (Arkes and Blumer 1985; Bowen 1987; Northcraft and Neale 1986; Northcraft and Wolf 1984; Staw and Ross 1987). By way of explanation, Northcraft and Wolf offer the insight that inappropriate project continuance will occur if the psychological benefits of continuing exceed the psychological costs of termination. In this context, the psychological benefits and costs include the monetary aspects noted earlier but also the individual and organizational advantages and disadvantages.

A number of researchers invoke the *sunk-cost* concept to explain the psychological costs and benefits by way of analogy (Arkes and Blumer 1985; Northcraft and Neale 1986; Northcraft and Wolf 1984). Reinforcement and utility theory both play roles in this concept. For example, reinforcement theory has found that random rewards will encourage people to continue a behavior well beyond the point that logic would dictate that their behavior has no effect on the rewards. And utility theory indicates that when some people have invested a significant amount in a risky situation, the potential loss of an additional increment of investment is much less valued than the potential gain from success.

Staw and Ross offer one of the most explicit discussions of the psychological reasons for inappropriate project continuance (1987). They categorize these reasons in terms of project aspects, managerial motivations, social pressures, and organizational forces. They also offer some advice to managers on how to avoid these psychological pressures.

Bowen indicates that it is important to formally *structure* an EPT decision in the project process, or else organizational commitment to the project tends to escalate for psychological reasons (1987). It seems clear that we are currently in a much more knowledgeable position to successfully initiate and implement EPT than we have been in the past. What is needed is a formal monitoring system that evaluates both project and organizational/individual factors for project viability, as well as inappropriate continuance. Such a system is proposed in the next section and incorporates the research results discussed earlier.

EARLY TERMINATION MONITORING SYSTEM

The system envisioned for initiating EPT consists of a monitoring function separate from the project manager's office. Ideally, this function should report to that level of the organization with the responsibility for initiating (and terminating) projects.

The early termination monitoring system includes audits in three major time frames. The first audit is a general organizational review, separate from any particular project and conducted at infrequent intervals, to determine the *personality* of the organization in terms of its susceptibility to inappropriate project continuance. This audit is then repeated as major personnel changes occur and over extended time spans when the direction and policies of the organization have changed through evolution.

The second audit time frame is immediately after initiation of every project. This audit considers both project factors and project personnel factors. The project factors to be considered at this stage are *static* in the sense that they reflect the project objectives and can be evaluated before progress is made.

The last audit time frame is ongoing during the project and repeated at regular intervals. This audit first considers the dynamic project factors that tend to change over time. While evaluating the dynamic project factors, the static factors are also reviewed for changes of relevance. Next, the audit analyzes the interplay that has occurred between the organizational factors and the project manager factors to date to determine if inappropriate project continuance may be occurring.

This process and the relevant factors are illustrated in Figure 1. The factors are measured on a five-point Likert-type scale and summed. The resulting sums can then be compare by the audit team or management across lines of business, across projects, or over time. Some of the factors in Figure 1, primarily in Step 1 and partially in Step 2, may be very difficult for internal auditors to evaluate; thus, it might be necessary for the firm to rely on external consultants or viewpoints. Also, the ongoing evaluation in Step 3B of the interaction of those factors in Step 1 with the factors in Step 2B might require the services of an unbiased outside observer.

It might also be noted that our focus with the factors here is on the termination decision, rather than possible changes to improve the chances of successful project completion. For many factors, such as changes in political forces or the firm's image, this is totally appropriate. However, other factors in Figure 1 may be amenable to change so as to improve the chances of a successful project. This should be considered as a possible alternative by the project team when making its report.

The first two steps in Figure 1 are prestartup and might be candidates for inclusion in the organization's formal project-approval process. A discussion of each of the steps follows.

Step 1: Organization Audit

The five items involved in the organizational audit as listed in Figure 1 are described here. The intent of this audit is to expose those high-scored elements of the organizational personality that tend to make it susceptible to inappropriate project continuance. A total score greater than fifteen should alert the audit team to the general possibility of future problems as well. The audit team can then check the potential for individual items to interact with particular projects and specific project managers to determine if inappropriate continuation may be occurring. As noted earlier, the organizational audit is repeated over time as seems appropriate to the changing personality of the organization.

Early Termination Monitoring System (ETMS)

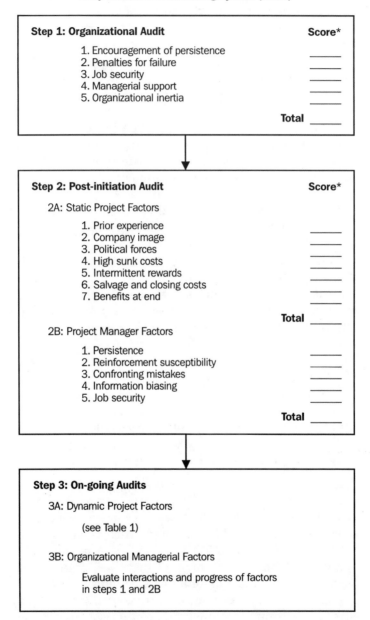

Step 1: Organizational Audit   Score*

      1. Encouragement of persistence   _____
      2. Penalties for failure   _____
      3. Job security   _____
      4. Managerial support   _____
      5. Organizational inertia   _____

                                    Total _____

Step 2: Post-initiation Audit   Score*

  2A: Static Project Factors

      1. Prior experience   _____
      2. Company image   _____
      3. Political forces   _____
      4. High sunk costs   _____
      5. Intermittent rewards   _____
      6. Salvage and closing costs   _____
      7. Benefits at end   _____

                                      Total _____

  2B: Project Manager Factors

      1. Persistence   _____
      2. Reinforcement susceptibility   _____
      3. Confronting mistakes   _____
      4. Information biasing   _____
      5. Job security   _____

                                      Total _____

Step 3: On-going Audits

  3A: Dynamic Project Factors

    (see Table 1)

  3B: Organizational Managerial Factors

    Evaluate interactions and progress of factors
    in steps 1 and 2B

*Score as a 1 if this factor presents no problem, up to a 5 if it presents a serious potential problem.

Figure 1   Process Flow of the Early Termination Monitoring System

1. Encouragement of persistence. Organizations often strongly encourage managerial persistence in the face of adversity. This characteristic may be inculcated in their employees without ever being recognized explicitly; yet, everyone knows it. Such persistence is often identified with strength and leadership in the managers, and promotions go to those who excel at it.

However, persistence in the continuation of a failing project wastes the organization's time, money, and other precious resources. Also, conditions can change such that a project once important to the firm's goals is no longer even relevant; to persist in the project is thus foolish. A common problem is that it may be difficult to tell if a project is failing, but persistence beyond the point when there is virtually no hope for success is wasteful.

2. Penalties for failure. Too often, the firm views failure with excessive disfavor. Heavy penalties for failure force managers to adopt one of two negative modes of behavior: unwillingness to accept even moderately risky projects or else refusal to give up on a project failure.

3. Job security. A corollary to the factor above is the amount of security that managers have in their jobs. If the firm's normal policy is to tie the job promotions or demotions to project success, then the negative managerial behaviors noted earlier will be common. The wise organization will attempt to provide managers with job security independent of their performance on specific projects.

4. Managerial support. Organizations must realize that if risk-taking is to be encouraged, then failures will be a natural consequence and must not be penalized. Instead, the support of top management is needed to encourage managers to continue to take such risks and make them realize that failure is not necessarily a reflection on their capabilities.

5. Organizational inertia. It is difficult for organizations to make changes, particularly changes reflecting negative outcomes. They tend to ignore information received and are reluctant to disrupt their standard, comfortable patterns of operation. Even more difficult is altering organizational policies, redefining jobs, or transferring people.

Step 2A: Post-Initiation Audit—Static Project Factors

The audit team can usually analyze this set of factors as soon as the project is adequately defined. The team conducts the audit soon after announcement or initiation of the project to determine anticipated weaknesses ahead of time, rather than after problems have arisen. If the total score on these factors exceeds twenty-one, the project should be reconsidered.

1. Prior experience. Does the firm have any prior experience in this or a related area? Without such experience, it is difficult to tell if problems that arise during the course of the project are serious or only temporary.

2. Organizational image. Sometimes a project becomes difficult to cancel because it is associated with the organization's *image.* Canceling the project might reflect badly on the entire organization. It is important to determine beforehand if a project is one of these types.

3. Political forces. Similar to the image problem noted above, strong political forces may be involved with continuing the project. Attempting to terminate a project in the face of such forces may bring undesirable excessive pressure on the organization.

4. Large sunk costs. A particular project may involve the expenditure of significant up-front or investment funds before any substantial progress is made. If so, the project has the potential for being inappropriately continued simply because of the extent of resources already invested in it. Clearly, the consideration of these sunk costs should occur before the investment is made—during project initiation—not during the EPT decision.

5. Intermittent rewards. If it appears that the project will be one with the potential for intermittent, random rewards, then the likelihood of inappropriate continuance through reinforcement theory must be considered. Forearmed, the organization can guard against believing progress is being made when the rewards come independently of any progress.

6. Salvage and closing costs. Akin to sunk costs, there may be reluctance to terminate a project because there is little salvage value in the project, or the costs of closing it down may exceed the immediate costs of keeping it going. Once again, it is better to consider these possibilities early, before the project gathers steam.

7. Benefits at the end. Some projects have the characteristic that all of the benefits come at the end of the project. If so, then there is great pressure to see the project through to the end, if only to recapture some of the sunk costs. Again, such a characteristic should be considered early, before progress makes termination unacceptable.

Step 2B: Post-Initiation Audit—Project Manager Factors

These factors, also conducted soon after project approval and appointment of the project manager, concern the characteristics of the project manager, particularly in relation to the personality of the organization. Again, the choice of the project manager should be reconsidered if the total score in this step is greater than fifteen.

1. Persistence. Does the project manager associate persistence with strength, leadership, and image? Are these characteristics important to her? Is withdrawal perceived as a sign of weakness? If so, the project manager may be playing right into the personality weakness of the firm, and inappropriate project continuance could easily arise.

2. Reinforcement susceptibility. Is the project manager likely to view random, successive project rewards as positive signs, or signs of progress? If the project is the type where this event is likely to happen, care must be exercised during project evaluation for continuance.

3. Confronting mistakes. Is the manager comfortable with the knowledge that everyone makes mistakes? Is he willing to face his own mistakes or admit errors of judgment? Or, is the manager likely to try to justify his own past behavior, or invest just a little more in the hope of turning around a failed project? What is the project manager's attitude toward risk, success, and failure?

4. Job security. Does the project manager feel secure about her career and job? Or does the manager worry that project failure may result in loss of the job as well? How accurate is this perception in terms of the organization's policies and history?

Step 3: Ongoing Audits

The third step is a qualitative one and requires detailed analysis of the project's progress and evolution to date, as well as insight concerning the interaction of the organization and the personality of the project manager. As noted earlier, this step may require the objective viewpoint of an outside expert or consultant. Considerable analysis is also necessary—thus, the absence of a checklist format for this portion of the early termination monitoring system.

Step 3A: Dynamic Project Factors

These audits are conducted on a regular basis over the lifetime of the project. The dynamic project factors are listed in Table 1 and have been synthesized from the literature described earlier on symptoms of project failure. The factors are dynamic in the sense that they change over the life cycle of the project, sometimes rather abruptly, and thus need to be constantly reassessed. The items listed in Table 1 are examples considered typical of that category.

1. Static factors. A review of the static factors is also needed at this audit to determine if any of these have changed for the worse. For example, the sunk costs may have been higher than were expected, or the salvage value may be less than was expected. To the extent that these have worsened, EPT may be more appropriate.

2. Task team. This set of factors concerns the nature of the task and the team conducting the project. In terms of the task, the audit should determine if the technical objectives have become more difficult to attain or if the technological or manufacturing problems are harder to solve than was expected. A clue to this difficulty is if the project milestones have frequently been missed so far, either in time or in terms of performance specifications. Another indicator is if the expected time to achieve the results seems to be stretching beyond earlier expectations.

The other side of this issue is the ability of the project team. Is it losing its enthusiasm? Has it become less innovative? Is its commitment dissipating? Clearly, technical problems can arise either because problems have become more difficult or because the team is less able to cope with them.

3. Sponsorship. The evaluation of this set of factors revolves around the commitment of the sponsor to the project concept. This commitment will be reduced if the project, for some reason, has become less consistent with organizational goals or less important to the firm in general. There may now be less of an expected impact on the firm, or the linkage with other projects the company is conducting may be weaker. Or, perhaps the opportunity or problem is reduced now. Or, possibly the project champion has been transferred or has taken another position. This will all be reflected in a reduced level of pressure to complete the project.

4. Economics. All of these factors center on the possibility of a reduced reward for the organization by completing the project. This can occur in a number of ways. The project's return on investment or sales, market share, or profit may be lower than initially expected. Or, perhaps there now appears to be a longer time to payback. Or, the cost to complete the project may now be considerably higher. This may be indicated, for example, through missed cost milestones to

1. **Review Static Factors**
   - Prior Experience
   - Company Image
   - Political Forces
   - High Sunk Costs
   - Intermittent Rewards
   - Salvage and Closing Costs
   - Benefits at End

2. **Task-Team**
   - Difficulty Achieving Technical Performance
   - Difficulty Solving Technological/Manufacturing Problems
   - Lengthening of Time to Completion
   - Missing Project Time or Performance Milestones
   - Lowered Team Innovativeness
   - Loss of Team or Project Manager Enthusiasm

3. **Sponsorship**
   - Project Less Consistent with Organizational Goals
   - Weaker Linkage with Other Projects
   - Lower Impact on the Company
   - Less Importance to the Firm
   - Reduced Problem or Opportunity
   - Less Top Management Commitment to Project
   - Loss of Project Champion

4. **Economics**
   - Lower Projected ROI, ROS, Market Share, Profit
   - Higher Cost to Complete Project
   - Less Capital Availability
   - Longer Time to Project Returns
   - Missing Project Cost Milestones
   - Reduced Match of Project Financial Scope to Firm/Budget

5. **Environment**
   - Better Alternatives Available
   - Increased Competition
   - Less Able to Protect Results
   - Increased Government Restrictions

6. **User**
   - Market Need Obviated
   - Market Factors Changed
   - Reduced Market Receptiveness
   - Decreased Number of End-Use Alternatives
   - Reduced Likelihood of Successful Commercialization
   - Less Chance of Extended or Continuing Success

Table 1 Dynamic Project Factors

date. Or, the financial scope may no longer match that of the firm, either because the resource availability is more problematic, or the relationship of the project cost to the rest of the budget is out of kilter.

5. Environment. The environment surrounding the project may have changed also, putting the project in jeopardy. For example, there may now be better ways of attaining the same results, such as through purchase or subcontracting. Or, perhaps competitors' reactions are more successful than expected. Another possibility is that it may now appear impossible to protect the project results with a patent or via trade secrecy. Or, possibly increased governmental restrictions have become a problem.

6. User. For any of a number of reasons, the market may be less receptive now. For example, the market need may have been relaxed, been obviated, or changed in some other way. Or, perhaps the relevant factors have changed. Or, maybe just the likelihood of success has fallen. Another aspect is that the number of alternative uses of the result may have dropped. Or, the extended success of the result may have decreased, even though the initial success is still assured.

Step 3B: Organizational/Managerial Factors

In this final step, the potential for psychologically interacting factors to foster inappropriate project continuance is addressed. The task facing the audit team is to analyze the managerial personality characteristics from Step 2B that might dovetail with any potentially inappropriate organizational policies in Step 1. If the team finds indications that such factors are beginning to affect project continuance, they are then investigated thoroughly. The team should specifically scrutinize issues of persistence, job security, and error justification since these areas hold the greatest potential for inappropriate project continuance.

In addition, the team should monitor other potentially dangerous effects as well. Examples would include information biasing by the project manager, the actualization of reinforcement theory, as described earlier, and organizational inertia. If these or other factors are found to be compromising the honest evaluation of the project, they must be followed up.

CONCLUSION

The termination of failing or nonviable projects is of major importance to organizations. Projects are becoming both more frequent and more expensive; the ability to save the resources commonly expended on failed projects is thus critical to organizational survival.

Research in project failure, its early symptoms, and the psychological reasons for organizational/managerial behavior now allow us to monitor for signs of inappropriate project continuance. By installing an early-termination monitoring system as described here, more of the precious resources wasted on nonviable and failing projects can possibly be saved and thereby, perhaps, the organization as well.

References

Arkes, H. R., and C. Blumer. 1985. The Psychology of Sunk Cost. *Organizational Behavior and Human Decision Processes* 35: 124–40.

Balachandra, R., and J. A. Raelin. 1980. How to Decide When to Abandon a Project. *Research Management* 23 (Jul.): 24–29.

Bowen, M. G. 1987. The Escalation Phenomenon Reconsidered: Decision Dilemmas or Decision Errors? *Academy of Management Review* 12.1: 52–66.

Buell, C. K. 1967. When to Terminate a Research and Development Project. *Research Management* (Jul.).

Dean, B. V. 1968. *Evaluating, Selecting, and Controlling R&D Projects.* New York: American Management Association.

Meredith, J. R. 1981. The Implementation of Computer Based Systems. *Journal of Operations Management* 2 (Oct.): 11–21.

Meredith, J. R., and S. J. Mantel, Jr. 1985. *Project Management: A Managerial Approach*, New York: Wiley.

Northcraft, G. B., and M. A. Neale. 1986. Opportunity Costs and the Framing of Resource Allocation Decisions. *Organizational Behavior and Human Decision Processes* 37: 348–56.

Northcraft, G. B., and G. Wolf. 1984. Dollars, Sense, and Sunk Costs: A Life Cycle Model of Resource Allocation Decisions. *Academy of Management Review* 9.2: 225–34.

Staw, B. M., and J. Ross. 1987. Knowing When to Pull the Plug. *Harvard Business Review* (Mar.–Apr.): 68–74.

Stewart, J. M. 1965. Making Project Management Work. *Business Horizons* (Fall).

Tadisina. S. K. 1986. Support System for the Termination Decision in R&D Management. *Project Management Journal* 27.5: 97–104.

Upgrade Your Project Management Knowledge with Leading PMI Titles

A GUIDE TO THE PROJECT MANAGEMENT BODY OF KNOWLEDGE (PMBOK® GUIDE) – 2000 EDITION

The Project Management Institute's (PMI®) PMBOK® Guide has become the essential sourcebook for the project management profession and its de facto global standard, with over 900,000 copies in circulation worldwide. It has been designated an American National Standard by the American National Standards Institute (ANSI) and is one of the major references used by candidates to study for the Project Management Professional (PMP®) Certification Examination. This new edition incorporates numerous recommendations and changes to the 1996 edition, including: progressive elaboration is given more emphasis; the role of the project office is acknowledged; the treatment of earned value is expanded in three chapters; the linkage between organizational strategy and project management is strengthened throughout; and the chapter on risk management has been rewritten with six processes instead of four. Newly added processes, tools, and techniques are aligned with the five project management processes and nine knowledge areas.

ISBN: 1-880410-23-0 (paperback)
ISBN: 1-880410-22-2 (hardcover)
ISBN: 1-880410-25-7 (CD-ROM)

SELLING PROJECT MANAGEMENT TO SENIOR EXECUTIVES

Janice Thomas, Ph.D., Connie L. Delisle, Ph.D. and Kam Jugdev

What's the secret to successfully selling project management to senior executives? You'll learn them all in this invaluable book. Through structured interviews and factor-analyzed survey results, the authors mix science and great writing with some of the profession's best advice to offer you new, practical and revealing tips on how to sell senior executives on the importance and benefit of project management in meeting strategic business objectives. Learn the art of successfully selling project management with Selling Project Management to Senior Executives: Framing the Moves that Matter...all the advice you'll ever need!
ISBN: 1-880410-95-8 (paperback)

THE CERTIFIED ASSOCIATE IN PROJECT MANAGEMENT (CAPM™) ROLE DELINEATION STUDY

This helpful book can answer many of your CAPM™ questions–and more! As project management grows in scope, importance and recognition, so do the related career options. Here, straight from The Project Management Institute (PMI®), is a look at the latest important global certification. The Certified Associate in Project Management (CAPM) certification lends professional credibility to men and women as they start their project management career path. This work tells the story of the development of the CAPM examination and outlines the knowledge a practitioner must master in order to pass the examination. Further, it offers a glimpse into the activities and responsibilities of CAPMs in the workplace. The Certified Associate in Project Management (CAPM) Role Delineation Study should be required reading for anyone who wants to pursue this certification.
ISBN: 1-880410-980-2 (spiral paperback)

THE FRONTIERS OF PROJECT MANAGEMENT RESEARCH

Dennis P. Slevin, Ph.D., David I. Cleland, Ph.D., Jeffrey K. Pinto, Ph.D., Editors

Tips from cutting-edge research that you can use now! Although humans have been managing projects for thousands of years, from roads and pyramids to the International Space Station, the organization of the activity into a profession has only evolved within the last 50 years. Formal research into the knowledge areas and processes required for successful projects is even more recent,

having begun in the early 1960s. This first-of-its-kind publication from the Project Management Institute (PMI®) brings together 28 research papers from internationally known and well-established researchers in project management from around the globe. From them you will glean an insightful overview of past and current research findings, and take an eye-opening excursion along frontiers fertile for future investigation. You will also find a wealth of practical information that you can use now in managing your projects, be they organizing meetings, producing new products, or building skyscrapers.
ISBN: 1-880410-74-5 (hardcover)

GOVERNMENT EXTENSION TO A GUIDE TO THE PROJECT MANAGEMENT BODY OF KNOWLEDGE (PMBOK® GUIDE) – 2000 EDITION

The secret to success in government is revealed. For those who make their living from national, regional or local government projects and want to avoid the costly and confusing chasms of bureaucracy, turn to the Government Extension to the PMBOK® Guide. It is a practical civics lesson for adults around the globe who want to succeed on government projects, not just endure them. If you are new to project management, pair this book with a copy of A Guide to the Project Management Body of Knowledge (PMBOK® Guide)–2000 Edition. If you're an experienced project professional wanting to venture into a new and lucrative direction, the Government Extension to the PMBOK® Guide may stand on its own or serve as a supplement to the PMBOK® Guide. Newcomer or veteran, you will be surprised that someone finally made government projects understandable! The authors are project practitioners from Africa, Great Britain, Japan, Mexico, South America and the United States who have packed the Government Extension to the PMBOK® Guide with sound, tested, generally applicable political advice and information. For example, you will learn the general principle behind why all government projects are begun, how to survive one-year budgets that you use or lose, and when selecting the lowest qualified bidder is not to your advantage. The Government Extension to the PMBOK® Guide teaches you how to get government jobs done right, on time and within budget. PMI turns political bureaucracy into practical and successful political sense.
ISBN: 1-930699-00-X (paperback)

PM 102 ACCORDING TO THE OLDE CURMUDGEON
Francis M. Webster Jr.

In this eagerly awaited follow-up to PM 101, Francis M. Webster Jr., a.k.a. the Olde Curmudgeon, offers a fascinating and very readable guide to getting your project right the first time. Among other issues, he discusses four aspects of quality in projects, the intricacies of risk management, and sixteen ways to reduce project duration. PM 102 is sprinkled with real-life examples and keen observations born of the author's forty-plus years in the project management field. Four subjects make this book unique. The discussion of the full range of resources available to you includes materials management and the effective use of executives and staffs of your organization. The clear distinction between the project and the product of the project provides a sharper focus on managing aspects of each. The discussion of quality provides a practical framework for minimizing "scope creep." The pragmatic discussion of reporting and control presents tested ways of ensuring that you know what is happening on your project, maintaining urgency throughout the project, and completing the project for a satisfied client.
ISBN: 1-880410-78-8 (paperback)

PROCEEDINGS OF PMI RESEARCH CONFERENCE 2002

The Project Management Institute (PMI®) Research Conference 2002, Frontiers of Project Management Research and Application, co-chaired by Dennis P. Slevin, Ph.D., Jeffrey K. Pinto, Ph.D., and David I. Cleland, Ph.D., held 14-17 July in Seattle, Washington USA, brought together top researchers and practitioners in the project management field. Their purpose was to discuss new learning, ideas and practices, as well as answer questions in areas that may still need more work. This publication brings their research to your fingertips. The evolution of any profession depends on the breadth and depth of its research. The baselines must be established and then tested. Ideas must grow and change to remain up-to-date with current issues and business practices in the world.
ISBN: 1-880410-99-0 (paperback)

PROJECT MANAGER COMPETENCY DEVELOPMENT FRAMEWORK

Sharpen your project manager skills now! Discover the career benefits of climbing into the Project Management Institute's (PMI®) new competency development framework. Like an evolving building's transparent superstructure, the competency framework enables you to clearly see the interdependencies between your job knowledge, skills and behavior. Readily uncover areas of outmoded or faulty construction and tackle only what needs renovating. Enjoy the clarity! Researched by senior-level PMI members for four years, The Project Manager Competency Development Framework has the primary purpose of sharpening the skills of project management practitioners everywhere. It also guides the professional development of aspiring project management practitioners. Organizations will find the framework useful in guiding practitioners to their fullest potential. Individuals will find the framework useful in guiding the development of their own project management competence against a recognized standard.
ISBN: 1-880410-97-4 (paperback)

QUANTIFYING THE VALUE OF PROJECT MANAGEMENT

C. William Ibbs, Ph.D. and Justin Reginato
William Ibbs, Ph.D. and Justin Reginato, from the University of California at Berkeley, explore real-world data from 52 U.S. corporations and find the key to a high return on investment. It is project management maturity. Mature PM departments have more on-time, under-budget projects; less variable schedules and expenses; and decreased cost ratios. Project management maturity benefits extend to the parent company where Dr. Ibbs finds lower utilization rates, higher production rates and lower operating costs. Dr. Ibbs shows how to assess PM maturity and track its development. If you are looking for a comeback to those who want proof of project management's corporate value, Quantifying the Value of Project Management lays out all the evidence you need.
ISBN: 1-880410-96-6 (paperback)

PROJECT MANAGEMENT INSTITUTE PRACTICE STANDARD FOR WORK BREAKDOWN STRUCTURES

PMI's first practice standard to complement and elaborate on A Guide to the Project Management Body of Knowledge (PMBOK® Guide) – 2000 Edition, this new manual provides guidance and universal principles for the initial generation, subsequent development, and application of the Work Breakdown Structure (WBS). It introduces the WBS and its characteristics, discusses the benefits of using a WBS, and demonstrates how to build a WBS and determine its sufficiency for subsequent planning and control. A unique feature is the inclusion of 11 industry-specific examples that illustrate how to build a WBS, ranging from Process Improvement and Software Design to Refinery Turn-around and Service Industry Outsourcing.
ISBN 1-880410-81-8 (paperback)

THE PMI PROJECT MANAGEMENT FACT BOOK, SECOND EDITION

First published in 1999, this newly enlarged and updated "almanac" provides a single, accessible reference volume on global project management and the Project Management Institute (PMI®). Topics include the history, size, explosive growth, and the future of the project management profession; parameters of the typical project; a statistical profile of the individuals working in project management based on recent, global research; the organizational settings in which project management activities take place; and valuable information about the world's largest professional association serving project management, the Project Management Institute. Appendices offer an additional wealth of information: lists of universities with degree programs in project management and PMI Registered Educational Providers; PMI's Ethical Standards; professional awards; a glossary; and an extensive bibliography. This is the central reference for those working in project management and a career guide for those interested in entering the profession.
ISBN: 1-880410-73-7 (paperback)

PEOPLE IN PROJECTS

Project management is fortunate in possessing a rich and growing body of tools and metrics that aid in helping us to more effectively run our projects. However, that is just what they are: tools and metrics. Project management is no less prone than any other discipline to the problems inherent in managing people. In fact, a strong argument could be made that project management offers far more

people problems than other forms of corporate activity because it can involve so many levels of tasks, deadlines, cost pressures, the need to accomplish work through teams, and the well-known challenge of helping employees who have great technical skills also develop their people skills. This important book, People in Projects, focuses on one of the nine knowledge areas of A Guide to the Project Management Body of Knowledge (PMBOK® Guide) – 2000 Edition: human resource management. It is a collection of some of the most important writing relating to the people side of project management that the Project Management Institute has produced in the last six years.
ISBN: 1-880410-72-9 (paperback)

PROJECT MANAGEMENT FOR THE TECHNICAL PROFESSIONAL
Michael Singer Dobson
Dobson, project management expert, popular seminar leader, and personality theorist, understands "promotion grief." He counsels those who prefer logical relationships to people skills and shows technical professionals how to successfully make the transition into management. This is a witty, supportive management primer for any "techie" invited to hop on the first rung of the corporate ladder. It includes self-assessment exercises; a skillful translation of general management theory and practice into tools, techniques, and systems that technical professionals will understand and accept; helpful "how to do it" sidebars; and action plans. It's also an insightful guide for those who manage technical professionals.
ISBN: 1-880410-76-1 (paperback)

THE PROJECT SURGEON: A TROUBLESHOOTER'S GUIDE TO BUSINESS CRISIS MANAGEMENT
Boris Hornjak
A veteran of business recovery, project turnarounds and crisis prevention, Hornjak shares his "lessons learned" in this best practice primer for operational managers. He writes with a dual purpose—first for the practical manager thrust into a crisis situation with a mission to turn things around, make tough decisions under fire, address problems when they occur, and prevent them from happening again. Then his emphasis turns to crisis prevention, so you can free your best and brightest to focus on opportunities, instead of on troubleshooting problems, and ultimately break the failure/recovery cycle.
ISBN: 1-880410-75-3 (paperback)

RISK AND DECISION ANALYSIS IN PROJECTS, SECOND EDITION
John R. Schuyler
Schuyler, a consultant in project risk and economic decision analysis, helps project management professionals improve their decision-making skills and integrate them into daily problem solving. In this heavily illustrated second edition, he explains and demystifies key concepts and techniques, including expected value, optimal decision policy, decision trees, the value of information, Monte Carlo simulation, probabilistic techniques, modeling techniques, judgments and biases, utility and multi-criteria decisions, and stochastic variance.
ISBN: 1-880410-28-1 (paperback)

EARNED VALUE PROJECT MANAGEMENT, SECOND EDITION
Quentin W. Fleming and Joel M. Koppelman
Now a classic treatment of the subject, this second edition updates this straightforward presentation of earned value as a useful method to measure actual project performance against planned costs and schedules throughout a project's life cycle. The authors describe the earned value concept in a simple manner so that it can be applied to any project, of any size, and in any industry.
ISBN: 1-880410-27-3 (paperback)

PROJECT MANAGEMENT EXPERIENCE AND KNOWLEDGE SELF-ASSESSMENT MANUAL
Based on the Project Management Professional (PMP®) Role Delineation Study, this manual is designed to help individuals assess how proficiently they could complete a wide range of essential project management activities based on their current levels of knowledge and experience. Included are exercises and lists of suggested activities for readers to use in improving their performance in

those areas they assessed as needing further training.
ISBN: 1-880410-24-9 (spiral paperback)

PROJECT MANAGEMENT PROFESSIONAL (PMP®) ROLE DELINEATION STUDY

In 1999, the Project Management Institute (PMI®) completed a role delineation study for the Project Management Professional (PMP®) Certification Examination. In addition to being used to establish the test specifications for the examination, the study describes the tasks (competencies) PMPs perform and the project management knowledge and skills PMPs use to complete each task. Each of the study's tasks is linked to a performance domain (e.g., planning the project). Each task has three components to it: what the task is, why the task is performed, and how the task is completed. The Project Management Professional Role Delineation Study is an excellent resource for educators, trainers, administrators, practitioners, and individuals interested in pursuing PMP certification.
ISBN: 1-880410-29-X (spiral paperback)

PM 101 ACCORDING TO THE OLDE CURMUDGEON

Francis M. Webster Jr.
Former editor-in-chief for PMI®, Francis M. Webster Jr. refers to himself as "the Olde Curmudgeon." The author, who has spent thirty years practicing, consulting on, writing about, and teaching project management, dispenses insider information to novice project managers with a friendly, arm-around-the-shoulder approach. He provides a history and description of all the components of modern project management; discusses the technical, administrative, and leadership skills needed by project managers; and details the basic knowledge and processes of project management, from scope management to work breakdown structure to project network diagrams. An excellent introduction for those interested in the profession themselves or in training others who are.
ISBN: 1-880410-55-9 (paperback)

THE ENTERPRIZE ORGANIZATION: ORGANIZING SOFTWARE PROJECTS FOR ACCOUNTABILITY AND SUCCESS

Neal Whitten
Neal Whitten is a twenty-three-year veteran of IBM and now president of his own consulting firm. Here he provides a practical guide to addressing a serious problem that has plagued the software industry since its beginning: how to effectively organize software projects to significantly increase their success rate. He proposes the "EnterPrize Organization" as a model that takes advantage of the strengths of the functional organization, projectized organization, and matrix organization, while reducing or eliminating their weaknesses. This book collects the experiences and wisdom of thousands of people and hundreds of projects, and reduces lessons learned to a simple format that can be applied immediately to your projects.
ISBN: 1-880410-79-6 (paperback)

FOR ADDITIONAL PMI TITLES, PLEASE VISIT AND SHOP OUR ONLINE BOOKSTORE AT WWW.PMIBOOKSTORE.ORG

Book Ordering Information

Phone: +1-866-276-4PMI for customers in North America
        +770-280-4129 for customers outside North America

Fax: +770-280-4113

Email: pmiorders@pbd.com

Mail: PMI Publications Fulfillment Center
        P O Box 932683
        Atlanta, GA 31193-2683 USA

©1999, 2003 Project Management Institute, Inc. All rights reserved.
"PMI", the PMI logo, "PMP", the PMP logo, "PMBOK", "PM Network", "Project Management Journal", "PMI Today", and the slogan "Building professionalism in project management" are all registered marks of the Project Management Institute, Inc."